PRODUCING A FIRST-CLASS NEWSLETTER

PRODUCING A FIRST-CLASS NEWSLETTER

A guide to planning, writing, editing, designing, photography, production, and printing

Barbara A. Fanson

Self-Counsel Press
(*a division of*)
International Self-Counsel Press Ltd.
Canada U.S.A.

Printed in Canada

First edition: February, 1994
Reprinted: May, 1996

Canadian Cataloguing in Publication Data

Fanson, Barbara A., 1959 –
   Producing a first-class newsletter

   (Self counsel reference series)
   ISBN 0-88908-296-0

   1. Newsletter — Publishing. I. Title. II. Series.
Z286.N46F35 1993   070.1'75   C93-091895-9

Cover photography by Terry Guscott, ATN Visuals, Vancouver, B.C.

Self-Counsel Press
(a division of)
International Self-Counsel Press Ltd.

Head and Editorial Office	*U.S. Address*
1481 Charlotte Road	1704 N. State Street
North Vancouver, British Columbia V7J 1H1	Bellingham, Washington 98225

To a wonderful friend and mentor, Nina Coco,
who always gives her time, attention, patience, and support
for which I'm forever grateful.
"Everything happens for a reason."

Contents

Introduction   xvii

Part 1
Planning: getting
your newsletter started

1   **What kind of newsletter do you need?**   3
   a.   What is a newsletter?   3
   b.   Kinds of newsletters   3
   c.   Know your readers   6
   d.   Forming objectives   6
   e.   Naming your newsletter   8

2   **Planning with a purpose**   10
   a.   Planning for consistency   10
     1.   How often will it be published?   10
     2.   Will your publication be distributed free
       or will there be a subscription?   11
     3.   What will your budget be?   11
     4.   What will the circulation be?   11
     5.   Who will provide the content?   11
     6.   What size will it be?   12
     7.   How many pages will it be?   12
     8.   When will it be published?   12
     9.   How will it be distributed?   12
   b.   Three categories for budgeting   13
   c.   Preliminary budget   14
     1.   Staff expenditures   14
     2.   Office space   14
     3.   Production   14
     4.   Distribution   14
     5.   Supplies   15
   d.   Choosing outside services   15
     1.   Hiring a writer   16
     2.   Hiring an editor   16
     3.   Hiring a proofreader   16
     4.   Choosing a printer   17
     5.   Hiring a designer   17

	6.	Hiring a desktop publisher	18
	7.	Hiring a photographer	18
e.	Start-up costs		18
f.	Typical charges		20
g.	Subscription newsletters		20
h.	Additional income		21
	1.	Mailing list rental	21
	2.	Advertising revenue	21
i.	Other financial considerations		23

Part 2
Format: setting a style

3	**Building a functional format**		29
a.	Why use a format?		29
b.	The grid system		31
	1.	Margins	32
	2.	Number of columns	33
	3.	Column width	35
	4.	Alley width	35
	5.	Headers and footers	35
	6.	Putting it all together	35
c.	Other formatting elements		38
	1.	Justification	38
	2.	Hyphenation	38
	3.	Widows and orphans	39
	4.	Paragraph style	39
d.	Using graphics in your format		40
	1.	Nameplate	42
	2.	Masthead	42
	3.	Calendar	42
	4.	Rules	46
	5.	Refers	47
	6.	Teasers	47
	7.	Continuation lines and jump lines	47
	8.	Ideograms	47
	9.	Initial caps	48
	10.	Table of contents	48
	11.	Standing heads	49
	12.	Pull quotes	50
e.	Bilingual publications		51

4 What you need to know about type   53

  a. The terminology of typography   53

    1. Serifs   53

    2. Leading or linespacing   53

    3. Kerning   53

    4. Type size   55

    5. Ascenders and descenders   55

    6. Typeface   55

    7. Type family   55

    8. Type style   56

    9. Type groups   56

    10. Character set   56

  b. Using type to enhance your message   56

    1. The personalities of type   56

    2. To serif or not to serif   57

    3. Choosing the right typeface   58

    4. Choosing the right size   59

    5. Headlines   59

    6. Caps and lowercase   59

    7. Adding emphasis   59

    8. Leading   60

  c. Character modification: adjusting typefaces   60

    1. Scaling and tracking   61

    2. Outlines and shadows   61

  d. Your type sheet   62

5 Color   64

  a. Do you need color?   64

  b. Low-cost color   65

  c. Choosing an appropriate color   65

  d. Full color through process printing   66

Part 3
Content: informing
and entertaining
the reader

6 The editor's role   71

  a. What does an editor do?   71

    1. Editorial advisory board   71

  b. Make your newsletter easy to read   71

    1. Using a readability index   71

    2. Edit for reading ease   72

  c. Working with contributors   73

		1.	Make sure they know what you want	73
		2.	Editing humanely	73
	d.	Style sheets		74
	e.	Purpose of a style manual		75
	f.	Preparing a style manual		78
	g.	ISSN (International standard serial number)		78
	h.	Legal deposit		79

7 The inside story — developing content — 80

	a.	The annual plan		80
	b.	Develop regular features		81
	c.	Use fillers		83
	d.	Content ideas		84
	e.	Using feedback		85

8 Good writing for great newsletters — 90

	a.	Writing styles		90
		1.	Inverted pyramid	90
		2.	Profile à la *Wall Street Journal*	90
		3.	The first person point of view	91
		4.	Extended dialogue	91
		5.	Question and answer	91
		6.	Interviews	91
		7.	Testimonials	92
		8.	A quiz	92
		9.	Practical tips	92
		10.	More articles, fewer columns	92
		11.	How-to information	92
		12.	Personal experiences	93
		13.	Exposes	93
		14.	Analysis	93
		15.	Point form	93
		16.	The great debate	94
	b.	Encourage reader participation		95
	c.	Quotations		95
	d.	Features to avoid		95
	e.	Story endings		96
	f.	Writing guidelines		96
		1.	Consider your audience	96
		2.	Know your subject	97
		3.	Adapt your style to fit your audience	98
		4.	Use constructions that make the meaning clear	98

	5. Grammar and usage	98
	6. Final checking	99
g.	Biased writing	99
h.	Increase the appeal of an article	100
	1. A startling fact	100
	2. An intriguing question	100
	3. A common myth	101
	4. Interesting anecdotes	101
	5. New information	101
	6. A slice-of-life	101
	7. Interesting comparisons	101
9	**Mechanics of writing**	**103**
a.	Grammar myths and misconceptions	103
b.	Grammar and spell checker software	103
c.	A few grammar rules	104
	1. Avoid verbs ending in "ize"	104
	2. Avoid slang	104
	3. Omit meaningless words	104
	4. Open, solid, and hyphenated terms	104
d.	Punctuating properly	105
10	**Writing headlines**	**108**
a.	Function of headlines	108
b.	Styles of headlines	108
	1. Banner headline	108
	2. Deck	108
	3. Kicker	109
	4. Hammer	109
	5. Slammer	109
	6. Tripod	109
	7. Raw wrap	109
	8. Sidesaddle head	109
c.	Writing effective headlines	110
d.	Tips for better headlines	110
	1. Promise readers a benefit	110
	2. News or announcement angle	110
	3. Numbers	111
	4. Using questions	111
	5. Secondary headlines	111
11	**Photographs**	**113**
a.	Elements of good photography	113

	b.	Photo sizing	113
	c.	Cropping photos	114
	d.	Photographic terms	114
		1. Cutlines	114
		2. Framing	114
		3. Flopping	116
		4. Reshaping	116
		5. Tilting	116
		6. Silhouetting	116
		7. Duotones	116
		8. Electronic photo manipulation	116

12 Legal considerations — 119

a. Copyright — 119
   1. What is a copyright? — 119
   2. Who owns the copyright? — 119
   3. How do you obtain copyright? — 119
   4. Should you register your copyright? — 120
b. Trade marks — 120
   1. What is a trade mark? — 120
   2. How do you differentiate trade marks from copyrights, industrial designs and patents? — 120
   3. What is a trade name? How is it different from a trade mark? — 120
c. Who owns artwork? — 120
d. Permission to reproduce photographs — 121
e. Previously published material and quotations — 124

13 Desktop publishing and some basic elements of design — 126

a. Desktop publishing — 126
b. DTP saves time and money — 126
c. Camera-ready copy from the computer — 126
d. Desktop publishing equipment — 127
   1. Central processing unit (CPU) — 127
   2. Color monitor — 127
   3. Laser printer — 130
   4. Label printer — 130
   5. Modem — 130
   6. Desktop scanner — 131
e. Desktop publishing software — 135
   1. Word processing programs — 135

2. Page layout programs 136

3. Graphics programs 136

4. Photo imaging programs 136

5. Database programs 136

6. Spreadsheet programs 136

7. Integrated programs 136

8. Accounting programs 136

9. Miscellaneous programs and utilities 136

f. Photo CD technology 136

g. Helpful hints for copyfitting 137

h. Using files from another computer 138

i. Elements of good design 139

j. Color, design, and content affect readability 139

k. Use visuals — PIGs 140

14 **Using traditional methods** 143

a. Copy preparation 143

1. Mark-up 143

2. Layout 143

b. Typesetting 143

1. The photocomposition process 146

2. Keyboard 146

3. Developing the images 146

c. Dry transfer method 146

d. Paste-up 147

e. Indicating color 147

f. Sizing artwork 149

g. Photo reproduction 149

1. Line copy 149

2. Continuous-tone copy 149

h. The process camera 149

i. Typesetting on photographs and screens 150

1. Surprint/overprint 150

2. Dropout/reverse 150

15 **Proofing** 152

a. The importance of proofing 152

b. Three proofing stages 152

1. From computer 152

2. From film 153

3. From printing plate 154

c. The proofreading process 154

    d.   Checking color proofs   157

16 Printing   160
    a.   Dealing with printers   160
    b.   Offset-lithography   161
    c.   Letterpress printing   161
    d.   Gravure printing   161
    e.   Screen printing   162
    f.   Paper selection   162
        1.   Printability   163
        2.   Colored stock   163
    g.   Bindery   163
        1.   Cutting   163
        2.   Collating   164
        3.   Drilling and punching   164
        4.   Stitching and stapling   164
    h.   Recycling   164

17 Distribution   168
    a.   Stuffing and sealing envelopes   168
    b.   Addressing   168
    c.   Postage   169
    d.   Other methods of distribution   169
        1.   Handouts   169
        2.   Piggybacks   170
        3.   Modem mix   170
    e.   Circulation   170

Worksheets

#1 What kind of newsletter do you need?   5

#2 Know your readers   7

#3 Objectives and goals   8

#4 Planning your newsletter   13

#5 Preliminary six-month budget   22

#6 Measuring your profit   24

#7 Newsletter specifications sheet   30

#8 Type sheet   63

#9 Annual plan   82

Samples

#1 Equipment costs   19

#2 Parts of a newsletter grid   31

#3 One-column newsletter   34

#4 Two-column newsletter   34

#5 Three-column newsletter   34

#6 Four-column newsletter   34

#7 Scholar's margin grids   36

#8 Typical one-column grid   37

#9 Typical two-column grid   37

#10 Typical three-column grid   37

#11 Typical four-column grid   37

#12 Graphic elements within a newsletter format   40

#13 Nameplate positions   43

#14 Mastheads   44

#15 Calendars   45

#16 Rules   46

#17 Initial caps   48

#18 Standing heads   49

#19 Pull quotes   50

#20 Bilingual newsletter   51

#21 Typographic terms   54

#22 Comparison of style manuals   76

#23 Readership survey   86

#24 Punctuating properly   106

#25 Cropping photographs   115

#26 Model release   123

#27 Desktop publishing equipment   129

#28 Basic design elements that aid readability   141

#29 Mark-up for typesetting   144

#30 Layout — mock-up   145

#31 Paste-up   148

#32 Proofreader's marks   155

#33 Proofread copy   156

#34 Imposition of a newsletter   165

Introduction

So you've been asked to edit and produce a newsletter for your organization. Or perhaps you want to initiate a newsletter to publicize your new business. You know that a well-designed, well-written newsletter can be an effective marketing tool and information source, and you want to do it right.

You're not alone. Today, newsletters are everywhere. The number of newsletters produced in North America has increased by a whopping 80% in the last ten years. The *Newsletter Directory*, published by Gale Research Company, estimates 8,000 newsletters are currently in print. This does not include house organs, publications of strictly local interest, and those distributed by hand. The 1987 *Oxbridge Directory of Newsletters* listed 13,500 newsletters, and *Hudson's Subscription Newsletter Directory* includes 4,570 subscription newsletters.

But newsletters aren't new. The first known examples were introduced by Count Philip Edward Fugger (1546-1618) of Augsburg, Germany. The loose, handwritten sheets reported business news gathered by several agents in trade centers around Europe and overseas. They became known as *Fugger-Zeitungen*. (Zeitung, which means tidings, later became the German word for newspaper.) These first publications had the basic characteristics of a modern newsletter: specialized information prepared for a specific audience.

The *Boston News-Letter*, published in 1704, was the first newsletter published in North America. Then, as newspapers and magazines grew in the 19th century, the popularity of newsletters began to decline. By 1900, newsletters began to bounce back. Many businesses and financial people were ready for more specialized news than they got from the mass media. There was a demand for the opinions of experts and forecasts of what might happen to their investments.

The first modern newsletter was the *Whaley-Eaton Report*, introduced in 1918. In 1923, Williard M. Kiplinger launched the *Kiplinger Washington Letter*. In 1980, his son, Austin, bought *Whaley-Eaton* and brought it into the Kiplinger organization. Williard Kiplinger is best known for inventing a style and format that has been widely imitated. The *Kiplinger Washington Letter* is a typewritten page with many underlines, ellipses, and fragmented sentences.

The newsletter industry has matured, according to Newsletter Association past president Thomas L. Phillips. During his keynote address at the 1987 Newsletter Association international conference in Washington,

D.C., Phillips noted that the novelty of the newsletter phenomenon is wearing off and newsletters are becoming legitimate in the eyes of government, the mass media, and the general public. Subscription renewals have increased and yesterday's hot new ideas are now established publications.

Newsletters have become increasingly popular in the United States, Canada, the United Kingdom, and Japan, where Nikkei-McGraw-Hill is launching Japanese newsletters and translating U.S. ones into Japanese.

Why have newsletters had such a rise in popularity? First, in a busy world they are quick and accessible. Very few people read everything in a newspaper or a magazine. Some read only certain sections. Newsletters can be read in a few moments in one sitting. Many people prefer to get their news in bite-size pieces.

Second, newsletters provide inside information. Businesses of all sizes and types have realized that newsletters are an effective but subtle form of promotion that can be used to deliver specific information to a particular audience.

With the arrival of desktop publishing, it is now faster, easier, and less expensive to produce a newsletter. Newsletter editors used to write the articles and a typesetting company or printing house typeset the copy and prepared the mechanical art. Today, many editors are writing and designing their newsletters with word processing and page layout programs on a personal computer. They can print out camera-ready artwork on a laser printer and deliver it to the printing house for production.

The power of the personal computer has given the editor far more control, but it has also meant that he or she must learn much more about the overall production of the newsletter, and that is where this book can help. In the following chapters, you'll learn how to organize, budget, schedule, edit, and produce a newsletter that you — and your organization — can be proud of. Also included are worksheets for the nitty-gritty of production: planning charts, specification sheets, assignment records, and more.

If you've never worked on a newsletter before, read the book through once to gain an overall picture of what you want to do and how to do it. Then, go back and refer to those sections that are most helpful to you and your organization. Keep the book near as you plan the first few issues of your newsletter. You may find you want to refer back to the sections on typography, editing, and using photos, for example. With the information provided in this book, you should have everything you need to put together an attractive, effective newsletter. The rest is up to you. Good luck!

Part 1
Planning: getting your newsletter started

1
What kind of newsletter do you need?

a. *What is a newsletter?*

In 1985, the *Encyclopaedia Britannica* finally included "newsletter" among its entries: "*newsletter*, informal publication, often simple in format and crisp in style, that provides special information for a defined audience. Newsletters are ordinarily but not always issued regularly. They offer varieties of personal journalism and seldom carry advertising."

Some of this definition could be applied to a newspaper or a magazine, so let's look at what distinguishes a newsletter from these other media.

The phrase "provides special information for a defined audience" is important. Unlike newspapers, newsletters are usually targeted at a very specific audience rather than at the general public. Because the content is more targeted, a newsletter should provide very specific information. The average person could go through the newspaper and read only a few articles in the whole publication because many are of little or no interest to him or her. In a newsletter, because the editor knows that the reader is a retail jewelry store owner, or an employee of Giant Corp, or has an interest in saving street children in South America, only articles of interest to that specific reader will be included. Therefore, the reader is far more likely to read most or all of the newsletter's contents.

But, you might argue, many magazines have equally specific audiences and subject matter. What, then, is the difference between a magazine and a newsletter? For one thing, the size of a newsletter is usually smaller than that of a newspaper or magazine. Any newsletter over 16 pages is considered a magazine. And, unlike magazines, newsletters do not have covers and are generally not as glossy. Larger budgets and more pages give a magazine increased flexibility in story lengths, color, and graphics.

Newsletters also have a different editorial style than magazines. Newsletter writing requires more focus and precision. As well, most newsletters do not carry advertising, both because it takes up too much space and because many believe that advertising affects the editorial integrity of the publication.

b. *Kinds of newsletters*

There are as many kinds of newsletters as there are businesses and organizations. The newsletter you will be publishing probably falls into one of the following categories:

- *Internal corporate newsletters* contain company news, promotions, profiles, upcoming events, and are distributed by the company to its employees.

- *External corporate newsletters* are a subtle form of promotion to clients and stockholders. Some articles may describe new products, profiles of satisfied customers, industry news, and applications.

- *Association publications* are distributed to members, suppliers, and media with news of meetings, profiles, and how-to information. The cost of the publication is usually included in members' dues. Forty-three percent of North American associations produce newsletters.

- *Organization newsletters* refer to publications issued by the government, labor unions, churches, clubs, and citizen organizations. Their objectives are awareness and education. Health and education organizations produce numerous newsletters to keep their donors and volunteers informed.

- *Public relations newsletters* are distributed by a company or association to prospective customers to tell them about a specific product or service. The newsletter is a form of promotion that provides information to the target audience to generate positive attention.

- *Multi-client newsletters* (also called generic newsletters) are written and produced for a group of clients. For example, one chiropractic newsletter can be used by several chiropractors in different cities or locations. A chiropractor buys the newsletter in bulk for customers with the chiropractor's name printed in the heading.

- *Subscription newsletters* are published regularly and sold to make a profit. They contain industry news, tips, profiles, how-to information, promotions, and features on a particular industry. Subscription newsletters depend on subscription revenues.

Like any new venture, publishing a newsletter should be thought out carefully before the first issue is even in the works. If you are starting a newsletter on your own initiative, you must determine what kind of newsletter you want to publish or is needed. If the job of newsletter editor has been handed to you by someone, you should take care to clarify exactly what is expected from the newsletter.

Often, people or organizations vaguely hope that a newsletter can be all things to all people. It is up to you to disenchant them. A newsletter designed for the employees of a corporation is a very different animal from one designed to sell products.

Use Worksheet #1 to help determine what kind of newsletter you will be publishing.

WORKSHEET #1
WHAT KIND OF NEWSLETTER DO YOU NEED?

Use the following questions to help determine what kind of newsletter you will be publishing. If you are publishing the newsletter yourself, answer the questions yourself. If the newsletter will be published by an organization or company, get the person or persons who assigned the newsletter job to you to help you answer the questions.

1. What is the primary purpose of this newsletter? (Some possible answers: to improve company morale; to sell more of our products; to educate the membership; to educate the general public; to improve our corporate image with the public)

    _____

    _____

    _____

    _____

    _____

    _____

2. Who is the primary audience for this newsletter? (Some possible answers: employees; customers; members; the general public)

    _____

    _____

    _____

3. Is this newsletter expected to make profit, to break even, or to be an expense?

    _____

    _____

    _____

    _____

4. Based on the answers given above, my newsletter will be this kind of newsletter (internal corporate, external corporate, association, etc.)

    _____

    _____

    _____

c. Know your readers

From Worksheet #1, you should have a basic idea of what kind of newsletter you will be producing. Now, you need to focus in a little more. Look at Worksheet #2 now and answer the questions in as much depth as you can. For example, in Worksheet #1, you determined who your audience is in general terms. Now, look closer at your readers. If, for example, your audience is "employees of Giant Corp," think about what kind of people work at Giant Corp. Are they primarily male, primarily female, or mixed? Are they mostly office workers or mainly warehouse workers? How old are they? Where do they live? Do they have children? Do they drive to work or use transit? When would they be most likely to take a few minutes to read a newsletter?

You may need to do some research to find out some of this information. If your organization is large, it may have some statistics to help you out. If not, or if the information you need is unavailable, you may need to do a survey or consult other resources.

d. Forming objectives

Knowing what kind of newsletter you will be producing is not enough. You still need to set specific *objectives* for your newsletter. For example, if yours is a public relations newsletter, your objectives might be to educate existing and potential clients, feature new applications, demonstrate the technical expertise of your staff, and show how the company is a responsible corporate citizen. Objectives are ongoing. You should review your newsletter annually or biannually to make sure that it is successfully reaching its objectives.

The *goals* of your newsletter should be more short-term, finite, and measurable. They should relate directly to the objectives. For example, if your objective is to demonstrate how the company is a responsible corporate citizen, one of your goals might be to run an article on the company's community involvement in every second issue for the next year. If your objective is to improve communication between members of a national club, one of your goals might be to get 95% of the membership reading the "Letters from readers" column within six months.

Use Worksheet #3 to set down your objectives and one or two goals that relate to each. The information you set down in Worksheet #2 should help you decide on some goals to achieve your newsletter's objectives.

WORKSHEET #2
KNOW YOUR READERS

OBJECTIVES AND GOALS

1. What are your readers like?

_____
_____
_____
_____
_____
_____
_____
_____
_____
_____

2. What do they need to know?

_____
_____
_____

3. What would they like to know?

_____
_____
_____

4. What motivates them?

_____
_____
_____

5. How can they benefit from the newsletter?

_____
_____
_____

WORKSHEET #3
OBJECTIVES AND GOALS

1. Objective_____
   Review date_____
   Goal_____
   Review date_____Achieved yes/no_____
   Comments_____

2. Objective_____
   Review date_____
   Goal_____
   Review date_____Achieved yes/no_____
   Comments_____

3. Objective_____
   Review date_____
   Goal_____
   Review date_____Achieved yes/no_____
   Comments_____

e. Naming your newsletter

Selecting an effective name for your newsletter is a vital part of defining what kind of newsletter it will be. Think about the image of your newsletter. Is a serious tone appropriate? Perhaps, if your newsletter is for clients of a financial service. Or, can you use a lighter approach? *Springboard* might be a good name for a newsletter from a diving association. Is the newsletter addressing people within an industry or specific field? Then its name might reflect a kind of "in-the-know" sophistication. Is the newsletter intended for the general public? In that case, its name should be understandable and accessible to anyone.

Most newsletter names identify the content or the publisher. *Newsletter Trends* describes the content, whereas *The Poodle Club of America News* identifies the publisher. The name should immediately bring to mind the subject or the source of the newsletter. It's okay to play on jargon or insider jokes if you are sure that everyone who receives the newsletter will understand — if your newsletter is for users of Knickerbocker's Pigment

Blender and you know that the machine is fondly nicknamed "the Knick" by its users, the title *Knick-Knacks* might be appropriate.

Short, original, lively names are easy to remember. Try playing with alliteration (*The Jones Journal* or *The Norwich Corp News*) and with names of commonly used objects associated with the company or organization (*Fishing Lines* for a seafood processor or *The Trowel* for a gardening club). Names like these are often followed by a subtitle or tagline that helps define the source or subject matter of the newsletter. For example: *The Trowel: The Newsletter of the Great Valley Gardening Club.*

If you are having trouble choosing a name, hold a brainstorming session with a few people involved in the publication. Consider all ideas at first, no matter how outlandish or off-base they may seem. Then, review your objectives for your newsletter, keeping in mind your audience. Narrow your choices down to three or four and make a considered decision from those.

DESCRIPTIVE WORDS FOR NEWSLETTER NAMES

Here are some words that are often used in newsletter names.

- accents
- advisory
- advocate
- alert
- almanac
- briefs
- briefing
- bulletin
- channel
- connection
- context
- digest
- dimensions
- eye
- examiner
- facts
- file
- focus
- forecast
- forum
- gram
- guide
- highlights
- horizons
- hotline
- ink
- insider
- interchange
- intercom
- journal
- keynote
- letter
- light
- line
- link
- list
- log
- monthly
- news
- notes
- outlook
- perspective
- post
- profile
- report
- reporter
- resources
- review
- scene
- scope
- spotlight
- survey
- tab
- times
- topics
- trends
- update
- viewpoint
- views
- voice
- weekly
- wire

2
Planning with a purpose

a. Planning for consistency

The key to producing a good newsletter consistently and on deadline is planning. Don't just throw together a first issue and get it out as quickly as possible for the sake of having a newsletter in existence. If you do that, your second and subsequent issues are likely to be very different as you learn from your mistakes made in haste. And every change you make as you blunder along will make your newsletter seem more and more inconsistent.

Remember, consistency is extremely important in a newsletter — consistency in format, content, design, and publishing schedule. Readers tend to like and feel comfortable with what is familiar. They like to pull a newsletter out of the envelope and recognize it immediately by the front page format. They like to turn to their favorite regular items. They like to be able to count on receiving an issue at a particular time. If your newsletter comes out sporadically, varies wildly in format, has no regular columns or items, and changes design with every issue, your readers will feel no emotional link to it and may not even recognize it.

So, now, before you even begin your first issue, stop. Think about the objectives and goals you determined in chapter 1 and consider some of the nuts and bolts issues you are going to have to make decisions on.

1. How often will it be published?

A newsletter should be published at least quarterly. Some of your other options are —

- every second month
- monthly
- bimonthly
- weekly

How often your newsletter should go out will depend on your budget, quantity of content, and whether there are outside considerations that will affect your publishing schedule.

You or the organization that is publishing the newsletter may not be able to afford a frequent publishing schedule. Since distribution costs often form a significant portion of the newsletter's total expenses, the more frequently it is published, the more often it has to be distributed, and the higher the annual costs. If yours is a small organization with few members or employees, a quarterly newsletter may be all you can afford or need. On the other hand, a large corporation or group might easily absorb the cost of a bimonthly or weekly publication.

The quantity of material you will have to work with will also be a factor in your decision. If you have the budget to hire freelance writers, you should be able to get as much material as you need, whenever you need it. However, few newsletter editors have that luxury. If you have to rely on volunteer contributions or write much of the copy yourself, you may not have the material to fill a weekly or bimonthly issue.

You may also have to deal with considerations such as reporting on specific events or putting out a calendar. If one of the primary purposes of the newsletter is to report on general monthly meetings, you may be bound to a monthly schedule. If, on the other hand, one of your primary functions is to remind members in a timely fashion of upcoming events and those events are happening weekly, you may need a weekly or bimonthly newsletter. In this case, you may want to put out a publication with fewer pages more frequently.

2. Will your publication be distributed free or will there be a subscription?

Your answers to Worksheet #1 in chapter 1 should tell you whether the newsletter will be a non-profit or for-profit one. However, perhaps your organization expects you to run a newsletter that, while not necessarily making a profit, will pay for itself in some way. Make sure this is clear.

3. What will your budget be?

How much money is your organization willing to spend on the newsletter? If you work for a business, your budget may be set by the customer relations department, the human resources department, or even the marketing department. Make sure you know who will be paying the bills and how much they are allocating. If the newsletter is for an association or club and is provided as a membership benefit, the group must decide how much of the membership fee is to go toward newsletter costs. For example, if the annual membership fee is $25, and the newsletter is monthly and costs $1 per issue to produce and deliver, the club will be spending almost half of each membership fee just for the newsletter. (For more on budgeting, see section **b.** below.)

Set your budget before you begin.

4. What will the circulation be?

How many copies of the newsletter are going to be distributed for each issue? Is that number more or less fixed (e.g., a corporate newsletter for employees where the number of employees doesn't vary much) or will you be expecting to increase that number?

5. Who will provide the content?

Do you have a budget to hire writers or will you be depending on volunteer contributions? Will certain members of the group (e.g., department heads, committee heads) be required to submit material on a regular basis?

Who provides the content will have a definite effect on your planning. Volunteer contributions are always difficult to plan for. Will anyone volunteer anything? Will they write it anywhere near the length requested? How much editing will it require? Will that then cut the length in half? Will they get it in on time or at all? Volunteer writers also need to be "jollied along" more than professionals or you will quickly find your source of content drying up!

6. What size will it be?

Approximately 80% of newsletters are a standard letter size of 8½" x 11". Some are printed on legal-size paper, 8½" x 14", but this is not very common in North America. The letter size is very practical for a number of reasons:

(a) Most readers are familiar and comfortable with this size of paper as they see it all the time.

(b) It is a standard size, which means printing costs will be less than if you chose an eccentric size.

(c) Whether mailed flat or folded, it fits into standard envelopes.

(d) Photocopiers handle this size as a matter of course.

(e) You have more options in layout with this size as opposed to a smaller size.

7. How many pages will it be?

Budget considerations or other factors may dictate that the newsletter have a certain number of pages. Many newsletters consist of one sheet, printed both sides. This would be a perfectly acceptable choice for you if it will accomplish your newsletter's objectives. Instead of establishing a fixed number of pages, you may prefer to work within a range — say four to eight pages. This gives you some flexibility while retaining a certain consistency.

8. When will it be published?

If you are dealing with a quarterly, will you publish in January, April, July, and October, or in March, June, September, and December? If it is important that Christmas events are announced in good time, perhaps a November issue will be necessary. If you are publishing monthly, you still need to decide whether your issues will be published at the beginning, middle, or end of each month.

9. How will it be distributed?

Will you be mailing out the newsletter? Leaving it in waiting rooms for people to pick up? Inserting it with invoices? Including it with paychecks? How the newsletter will be distributed is a consideration when deciding its size, how it will be folded, and its format. It will also affect your budgeting, as mailing can be an expensive method.

Now complete Worksheet #4 with your answers to the above questions.

WORKSHEET #4
PLANNING YOUR NEWSLETTER

Answer these questions to plan your newsletter:

1. How often will it be published?

_____

2. Will your publication be distributed free or will there be a sub-scription?

_____

3. What will your budget be?

_____

4. What will the circulation be?

_____

5. Who will provide the content?

_____

6. What size will it be?

_____

7. How many pages will it be?

_____

8. When will it be published?

_____

9. How will it be distributed?

_____

b. Three categories for budgeting

For budgeting purposes, newsletters can be classified into three categories: corporate, non-profit, and commercial. The income and expenses generated by these three types of newsletters will vary.

The writing and production expenses for corporate newsletters are usually considered to be promotional or marketing expenses. An organization may opt to distribute a newsletter to prospects as a means of educating, informing, or persuading the client. If the organization is selling high-ticket items, it may produce a glossy, more expensive newsletter.

Associations may produce a non-profit newsletter to inform members of upcoming events or changes in the industry. Membership fees or advertisement sales will pay for the production and distribution of the newsletter.

Commercial newsletters, such as subscription newsletters and multiclient newsletters, must generate revenue to publish, distribute, and promote the publication. The amount of revenue will dictate how much money can be spent on writers, designers, printing, and distribution. In turn, the quality of the publication and the amount of promotion will determine the number of subscribers.

c. Preliminary budget

It is important to set a preliminary budget for your newsletter, as it will help you determine how much you can spend on writing, designing, and printing. These estimates are rough guesses until you have produced your first issue and find out exactly how much it will cost. When setting up your budget, here are a few things to consider.

1. Staff expenditures

If you are part of an in-house department and only a portion of your time is spent on newsletter publishing, calculate how much of your time it takes up. You will have to calculate this for each person involved in the production of the newsletter. This calculation should include salaries and benefits. Outside services such as writing, design, and production are covered below.

2. Office space

Do you lease an office, or work from your home? You must calculate the cost of rent or space allocation. Include utilities, telephones, fax, and other office equipment such as photocopiers.

3. Production

Production costs usually represent the highest costs of publishing a newsletter. Your estimate should include the costs of on-site equipment such as computers and typewriters. Also include outside supplies that you have to pay for, such as typesetting, graphic designers, photographers, paste-up artists, halftones, etc. Make sure outside services are worth the cost. For example, if you are producing 500 copies, expensive design costs may be extravagant. Otherwise, if a good-looking newsletter will help generate business, the costs may be worth it.

You can get an estimate for printing and binding from a print shop based on the number of copies and the frequency of your newsletter. You may want to get quotations from three printers and choose the best deal with the best quality and service.

4. Distribution

How will you get your newsletter into the hands of a reader? Can you use inter-office mail or will your newsletter be mailed? Do you have enough copies to qualify for reduced bulk mail rates? Is your mailing list sorted according to postal or zip codes? Will your newsletter be enclosed in an envelope?

Include in your budget the cost of envelopes and stuffing the envelopes. Is your newsletter a self-mailer with postal indicia printed on it? Have you discussed newsletter distribution with your local postal representative to determine the best rate?

5. Supplies

Include all on-site supplies such as paper for computers, typewriters, and photocopies; ribbons and toner cartridges; and all miscellaneous supplies such as pencils, pens, writing pads, and paper clips.

Leave room in your budget for unexpected expenses.

Whenever possible, overestimate. Your actual expenditures will probably be much greater than you originally calculated. Consider and allow for the cost of the following items when you plan your budget:

- Writer
- Editor
- Art director
- Designer
- Desktop publisher
- Illustrator/photographer
- Typesetting
- Proofreading
- Secretarial/typing
- Critiques/evaluation
- Software/supplies
- Copying/stats
- Paste-up
- Printing
- Mailing
- Postage
- Distribution
- Delivery charges/storage
- Staff time
- P.R. firm or ad agency

d. Choosing outside services

If you don't have the time or the specialized skills to produce an entire newsletter yourself, you might want to hire a skilled freelancer. Here are guidelines for dealing with and paying for services performed by someone outside your organization.

1. Hiring a writer

You can hire a writer to write the articles for your newsletter. Before each issue, spend time with the writer to establish story ideas for the next issue. (See chapter 6 on dealing with writers.)

You can pay a writer an hourly rate, by article or column, or a negotiated per-newsletter fee. The average rate for a writer is $200 to $400 per page for a two- to four-page newsletter; the four- to eight-page rate is $500 to $1,000. The per hour rate varies from $20 to $60. Rates may vary depending on geographic location and the state of the economy.

A standard 8 ½" x 11" newsletter has approximately 800 words of body text per page. This will vary depending on your page design and the typeface you are using. If you want two articles per page, then you could pay the writer to write a 400-word article for an established rate.

Avoid signing any long-range contracts with your writer until you feel comfortable with the writer's work and your ability to judge the quality. Some newsletter publishers give their writers a share of the profits as an incentive. A 5% profit to your writer for each subscription renewal is only $1.20 of a $24-per-year newsletter. If the writer is good, you get to keep the customer for another year.

2. Hiring an editor

A professional editor can contribute to a professional newsletter.

After your newsletter has been written, it should be edited for spelling and grammatical errors, sentence structure, clarity of expression, consistency, and organization.

Someone other than the writer should edit the newsletter. If your budget does not allow for hiring an editor, ask a friend or associate to perform this function. If you hired a writer, perhaps you can act as the editor.

The hourly rate for an editor is $12 to $50. Some editors are paid a flat rate of $15 per page. Rates vary depending on your locale and the experience and qualifications of the editor.

Make sure your editor reviews past issues of the newsletter and understands your philosophy, content, mission statement, and target market.

3. Hiring a proofreader

A proofreader reads final copy, or proof, to detect errors. A family member or a friend may have the skills and interest in this position, or you can advertise for a part-time proofreader. Proofreaders charge $7 to $25 per hour. Choose someone who can work within your time frame. It is best not to have the writer or editor proofread the work. Since the writer and editor are involved in content, style, and flow of information, they may let minor mistakes slip by.

Be sure to discuss duties and deadlines with the proofreader. Proofreading is discussed in more detail in chapter 15.

4. Choosing a printer

Printing shops vary in the quality of their work, the services offered, and the prices charged. Some printers do two-color printing, which means black plus one spot color. Others do four-color printing. Some printers have a variety of bindery and finishing equipment to complete the work. Other printers farm out binding. Some printers specialize in business stationery or business forms or books.

At least one month prior to printing, discuss your project with a printer. Ask questions such as how many days will it take to print and fold your newsletter? Obtain at least three quotations for printing your newsletter. Compare prices and look for quality. You may get a better printing price in another city, but if it takes two hours to drive there, you're not really saving. Ask to see samples of their recent work. Does it look professional? Is the printing clear? Does it have messy ink spots, hickeys, smudges, or tears in the paper?

You can save money by purchasing paper in bulk and storing it at the print shop. Avoid buying paper in bulk until you have had a few newsletter issues printed.

Evaluate your print job:

- Is it the ink color right ?

- Is it the paper color right?

- Is there overprinting or underprinting?

- Are there smudges on the finished job?

- Was the correct number of issues printed?

- Did the printer deliver on the date promised?

- Does the invoice agree with the quotation from the printer?

5. Hiring a designer

You may wish to hire a designer to design the original newsletter with guidelines for point size, typeface, grids, and overall page design. When hiring a designer, be specific about how you want the design presented. It could be supplied as templates with style sheets in the computer program of your choice, or it may be presented as hard copy only. It could also be presented as a marker rendering. What are you expecting the designer to create: page and type design, nameplate, standing heads, or logos? Be specific.

Most designers charge by the hour or by the project. Make sure you get a written estimate and establish a deadline for completion of the required design elements. Hourly design fees range from $20 to $100 per hour, depending on the reputation of the designer and how much creativity is required. Outside supplies and materials are usually extra charges. Designers usually mark-up outside supplies such as printing by 10% to 35%.

A designer can also be used on an ongoing basis to layout your pages.

6. Hiring a desktop publisher

Some desktop publishers are creative and can design attractive newsletters, others stick to the typesetting and layout of the publication on a regular basis. When hiring a desktop publisher, ask to see samples of recent work. Producing color on a desktop computer is not easy and is often performed incorrectly. Make sure the desktop publisher isn't taking on more than he or she is capable of. Does the desktop publisher know about trapping and overprinting? These terms are discussed in more detail in later chapters.

An art director I know spent $13,000 at a service bureau because he hired a desktop publisher to produce a color brochure with several logos. The brochure looked beautiful on the computer monitor, but the desktop publisher didn't produce color separations, so the service bureau had to do it. If four-color work is expected, make sure you're supplied with the original file, as well as color separation files.

Most desktop publishers charge an hourly rate of $20 to $100 per hour. Outside supplies and materials are extra. Like designers, desktop publishers mark-up outside expenses by 10% to 35%.

Do you want a diskette supplied? Do you want laser printouts or imagesetting on paper or film? If you're supplied negative film for four-color newsletters, do you require overlay proofs or laminated proofs? Desktop publishing is discussed in detail in chapter 13.

7. Hiring a photographer

Like other creative services, you must be specific when dealing with photographers. What do you want them to supply?

A photographer may charge a location fee for traveling to the photo shoot. Professional photographers will not supply negative film, but will probably give you a contact sheet made from the negatives that shows all the photos. Pick out the ones you want produced and the photographer will charge for each print for one-time use only. Rates will vary depending on color or black and white, and the desired size of the print.

Location fees could be a flat rate and an additional hourly rate for the photographer's time. My photographer charges a location fee of $75, plus an hourly rate of $25 for labor, plus $50 for each 5" x 7" black and white photograph. All photographs are for one-time use only.

e. Start-up costs

Whether you want to start a commercial newsletter for profit, produce a newsletter for others, or start a company newsletter, you will need equipment and supplies to get started. Start-up equipment costs have been divided into low-end, middle range, and high-end depending on what role you will play in the production process. Sample #1 outlines basic equipment needs for low-end to deluxe jobs. You may be handling a portion of the writing and production, or you may be handing the entire project. What equipment will satisfy your needs today and tomorrow? What office or production supplies are needed? Will you need additional furniture? Do you need a photocopier?

The following is a list of basic equipment for starting your newsletter:

- Computer
- Software — word processing, page layout, graphics, photo imaging, circulation, database, type fonts
- Desktop scanner
- Laser printer
- Laser paper, toner
- Label printer, labels
- Other peripherals
- Typewriter
- Photocopier
- Postage meter
- Envelope stuffing machine
- Desk/computer table
- Filing cabinet
- Light table
- Telephone
- Fax machine
- Answering machine

SAMPLE #1
EQUIPMENT COSTS

Equipment needs are based on your product/service and your budget. Computer and equipment prices change frequently.

	Low-end	Intermediate	Deluxe
Job function	Word processing writing	Desktop publishing basic graphics instruction	Desktop publishing signage, color publications, training
Computer	Basic, low-end	Intermediate	high-end with color
Monitor	Black & white	Color	Color
Keyboard	Regular	Extended	Extended
RAM/storage	2 MB RAM	5 MB RAM	8 MB RAM
	40 MB hard drive	80 MB hard drive	230 MB hard drive
Printer	Ink-jet or laser	Laser	Laser
Scanner	Not necessary	300 dpi color	600 dpi color
Modem	Not necessary	9600 baud modem	1440 baud fax/ modem
CD-ROM	Not necessary	Not necessary	Yes
External drive	Not necessary	Not necessary	88 MB removable
Data converter	Not necessary	Not necessary	Optional
Answer mach.	Yes	Yes	Yes
Fax machine	Yes	Yes	Yes

f. Typical charges

If you hired a design firm to produce a four-page newsletter, the cost breakdown might resemble this:

Writers	$100 per 400-word article	800
Editor	$25 per hour	100
Photography	$50 per 5" x 7" photo	200
Design/Desktop Publishing/Scanning		
	$50 per hour	300
Optional: Halftones, PMTs		
	$6 per print	12
Proofreading	$20 per hour x 2 hours	40
Imagesetting (1270 dpi output)		
	$12/page x 4 pages x 2 colors	96
Printing	2,000 copies, 2 ink colors	450
No. 10 Envelopes	For distribution, one color	125
Mailing house	$15/1,000 (stuffing, labels)	30
Postage	For 2,000 newsletters	860
Total Expenses for four page newsletter		**$3,013**

Depending on the quality and budget of your newsletter, some of these expenses are optional.

For example, if you are writing all the articles, then you won't have to pay for a writer. If the newsletter is produced for promotional purposes, then you will want to pay for professional writing. If there are no photographs or screened boxes, you could print directly from the laser proofs rather than pay extra for imagesetting. Again, it depends upon the quality you produce.

g. Subscription newsletters

Subscription newsletter publishers rely on subscription sales to cover costs of producing and promoting the product. Many newsletter publishers sell books, directories, special reports, and other ancillary products to supplement their income.

For example, Sterling Communications Inc. produces a subscription newsletter called *Newsletter Trends* and distributes it each month to subscribers. The newsletter discusses writing, editing, design, photography, and printing. Because the how-to newsletter is marketed to newsletter editors, the editorial content and design of each issue must be top-notch, or readers won't renew their subscriptions at the end of the term.

Most of the writing and production of *Newsletter Trends* is done in-house on a Macintosh computer using Microsoft Word and QuarkXPress. Some outside experts are hired to complete the publishing functions, as well as add credibility to the newsletter.

Sterling Communications produces artwork for other organizations, as well as *Newsletter Trends*. The subscription newsletter represents about one-quarter of company revenues and time, so a portion of rent and utilities must be calculated. Monthly expenses include:

Managing editor/writer	($50 per hour x 8 hours)	$400
Desktop publishing	($60 per page x 8 pages)	480
Additional columns/articles		180
Photography	($50 per 5" x 7" photo)	100
Proofreading		53
Imagesetting (1270 dpi paper — $12/spread x 4)		48
Printing (8 pages, black ink plus 1 spot color)		265
Hand-folding newsletter for envelope (2 hours)		40
Stuffing envelopes/apply labels (2 hours)		40
Postage		86
Office rent		81
Telephones/fax		25
Portion of computer equipment lease		109
Office supplies (paper, toner cartridge, etc.)		14
Monthly expenses		**$1,921**

Monthly expenses of $1,921 x 12 months = $23,052 per year. A subscription to the monthly publication is $85, so the publisher needs at least 272 subscriptions to break even. Don't forget the promotional costs of getting subscriptions, administration and circulation expenses, and getting renewals. To work out your own budget, see Worksheet #5, which sets up a preliminary budget for a six-month period.

h. Additional income

1. Mailing list rental

If you have a database of readers, you could generate additional revenue by renting out your mailing list for a one-time use of 15¢ to 50¢ per name. Contact a direct mailer or mailing service for additional information. Your mailing list should be versatile and have the ability to sort in a variety of ways. In database software programs, each name and address is called a record. If you have 200 readers, you probably have 200 records. Each piece of information is called a field. For example, Mr. John Smith would use three fields: one each for title, first name, and last name. Your database can be sorted according to city, male readers only, or occupation, depending on how much information you saved with each record. The more fields of information, the more thorough your database, and the more mailing list rental revenue you could earn.

2. Advertising revenue

To help defray production and distribution costs, your newsletter could sell advertising space. Related businesses might want to promote their

WORKSHEET #5
PRELIMINARY SIX-MONTH BUDGET

Frequency	Jan.	Feb.	March	April	May	June
Staff expenditures:						
Salaries						
Benefits						
Office space:						
Rent/Lease						
Utilities						
Telephone/Fax						
Photocopier						
Other						
Production/on-site:						
Computers						
Printer						
Typewriters						
Production/outside:						
Writing						
Design						
Photography						
Typesetting						
Paste-up						
Halftones, PMTs						
Service bureau/ film house						
Printing						
Distribution:						
Mail services						
Postage						
Envelopes						
Other delivery						
Supplies:						
Computer/typewriter/ copier paper						
Ribbons/toner						
Miscellaneous						
Notes:						

products or services to your defined readers. Many subscription newsletters will not accept advertisements, because subscribers have paid for eight pages of information, not advertising. You could consider inserting brochures or flyers into your mailing envelope for a fee per envelope. Some editors frown on this practice because they fear paid advertisements could ruin their editorial integrity or bias-free credibility.

Items to consider with advertising sales:

(a) What businesses could benefit by advertising in the publication?

(b) Who will sell the advertising space?

(c) Do we need an advertising contract?

(d) Will we charge extra for production of the advertisement, or should ads be supplied camera-ready?

(e) What is the deadline for advertising sales?

(f) What is the deadline for supplied advertisements?

(g) Will we charge extra for spot color on the ad?

(h) Will we charge extra for preferred positions, such as the back cover or inside front cover?

(i) How much do similar publications charge for advertising space?

To calculate advertising rates use this formula:

Total Production Costs ÷ Number of Pages = Cost Per Page

A full-page advertisement could be the cost of one page in the newsletter. For example, a four-page newsletter costs about $2,983 to produce. According to the formula: $2,983 ÷ 4 pages = $745.75

Your advertising rates could be the following:

- Full page ad — $750
- Half page ad — $400
- Quarter page ad — $225
- One-eighth page ad or business card — $150

You probably won't sell many full-page advertisements, but you may sell many one-quarter or one-eighth page ads. Any ad sale will help pay production costs of publishing a newsletter. A word of caution: don't sell too many ads. After all, you don't want to turn off a reader by having too many ads.

Instead of advertising space in your newsletter, an advertiser might consider inserting a brochure or flyer in your mailing envelope. The message still reaches the reader, and it doesn't take up valuable editorial space.

i. Other financial considerations

Don't forget to include sales tax in your budgeting, if it is applicable in your area. As sales tax rules are different for each state and province, consult the appropriate authorities in your area for a complete explanation of the taxes you will be liable to pay. In some areas, certain organizations and products may be tax exempt. Use Worksheet #6 to measure your newsletter's progress in terms of profit.

WORKSHEET #6
MEASURING YOUR PROFIT

MEASURE YOUR NEWSLETTER'S PROGRESS

Newsletter_____ Year _____

	Month			Year to Date (months)			
	Average Last Year	Budget This Year	Actual This Year	Actual Last Year	Budget This Year	Actual This Year	% Change vs. Last Year
1. Receipts New subs Renewals Back copies Other							
2. Editorial Salaries/fees Telephone Misc.							
3. Publishing Print, mail Postage							
4. Promotion Direct mail Space ads Other							
5. Gen. & Admin. Salaries, rent Legal, Acctg. Office, postage Payroll tax Insurance Bus. machines							
6. Total Expenses							
7. Profit							

8. Verification   Add: [ ]
     Cash balance, end of prev. month: [ ]
     = Cash balance, end of this month: [ ]

If, after working on your budget you still need to find ways to save money, use some of these cost-cutting tips:

- Fewer pages, fewer copies, or fewer issues per year will reduce costs.

- If you know another publisher, pool supplies and services.

- Take your own photographs.

- Use photocopiers with enlargement and reduction features instead of sending material to a printing house for expensive reproduction services.

- "Gang" photographs. If all your photographs are going to be the same size, they can be made into "halftones" (see chapters 11 and 14 for a definition of terms and details) at the same time to save money.

- Do your own paste-up or desktop publishing.

- Avoid bleeds, tight registrations, and other specialty printing problems.

- Talk to other editors or publishers. Perhaps they can suggest ideas on reducing costs or publishing a newsletter more efficiently.

THE TEN MOST COMMON REASONS NEWSLETTERS AREN'T READ

1. Unattractive appearance
2. Boring headlines that don't offer benefits
3. Too much type and not enough art
4. Not distributed to the right audience
5. Typographical errors or too many errors
6. Writing style does not suit readership — too much jargon or too simple
7. Articles do not interest the reader
8. Looks too amateurish and isn't taken seriously
9. Lacks "color" or graphics
10. Uninteresting or ineffective articles

There's nothing worse than realizing that your message is not getting through. Here are ten reasons why newsletters are ignored by readers.

Part 2
Format: setting a style

3
Building a functional format

Good typographic design and layout help get the printed message from the page to the reader. Anything that interferes with this is a mistake.

As the designer of your newsletter, you have two functions: to produce an attractive, appealing product that people will want to read and to help them read it. Everything about the newsletter — format, design, typestyle, artwork, headlines — must work together to attract a reader and compete with the hundreds of visual printed materials that readers see every day.

a. Why use a format?

The first thing you must determine is the format of your newsletter. Format refers to those elements of your newsletter that are consistent from issue to issue — size, number of columns, typestyle, type size, etc. Together, these elements will make up a standard look for the newsletter. This look should be consistent and distinctive, yet allow for creative design within each issue. Therefore, your goal should be to create a format that will provide guidelines and boundaries without being rigid and boring.

A recognizable format maintains consistency among issues. It also helps readers find information simply and quickly. Familiarity aids in developing readership and loyalty. Having a standard format will also save you time and money because every issue will start with certain predetermined parameters. You won't have to decide every issue which typestyle and size to use, or how many columns are best.

Many of your formatting decisions should be expressed in printers' measures rather than inches or centimeters. This is standard in the print publications industry, so you should familiarize yourself with the most common measures, picas and points.

One *pica* is equal to ⅙ of an inch; there are six picas to one inch. One *point* is equal to ¹⁄₁₂ of a pica; there are 12 points in one pica, and 72 points equal one inch.

Type sizes are usually expressed in points (e.g., nine-point type). Column widths and other larger sizes are usually expressed in picas (e.g., two-pica alley, 28-pica column). A special printer's ruler called a *pica gauge* (sometimes called a *pica pole*), which is marked in picas and points, is available from graphic supply stores. Using one will make the transition to printer's measure easier for you.

As you work through your formatting decisions, make notes on what you decide. When all your formatting is in place, use Worksheet #7 to

WORKSHEET #7
NEWSLETTER SPECIFICATIONS SHEET

PLANNING YOUR NEWSLETTER

1. Format (size) _____

2. Grid (number of columns)_____

   Margins (top, sides, bottom) _____

   Line length _____

   Alley _____

3. Nameplate (name and position)_____

   _____

4. Headlines (typestyle) _____

   Primary stories (type size and style) _____

   Secondary stories (type size and style) _____

   Fillers (Optional)_____

   Subheads _____

   Style: CAPS *or* U/lc *or* CAP first letter only _____

5. Body copy (typestyle) _____

   Justified *or* flush left/ragged right_____

6. Paragraph treatment

   Indent (How much?) _____

   or Space between (How much?) _____

7. Captions (typestyle and placement) _____

   _____

8. Masthead (typestyle and placement)_____

   _____

9. Page numbers (typestyle and placement)_____

   _____

10. Rules (line thickness and placement)_____

    _____

    Additional notes _____

    _____

    _____

    _____

    _____

    _____

    _____

record your newsletter's specifications. When you begin designing your first issue, you can refer back to this sheet for your basic format.

In chapter 2, you began to think about the size of your newsletter. This is your first formatting decision. Once you have clear in your mind what size you will be working with, you can move on to your other format decisions.

b. The grid system

Most magazine pages are designed with a grid: a matrix of non-printing lines that assist in the placement of certain elements on a page. When developing a grid, you must decide the width of left and right margins, top and bottom margins, the number of columns, the width of columns, and the width of the "alleys" between columns. A grid can also be used to place repeating elements including headers, footers, page numbers, and vertical and horizontal rules. A grid provides consistency from page to page and from issue to issue. It also develops and maintains appealing proportions. Sample #2 shows the parts of a newsletter grid.

SAMPLE #2
PARTS OF A NEWSLETTER GRID

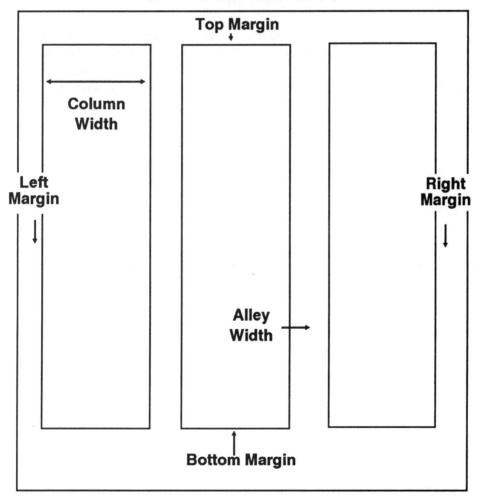

1. Margins

You have left, right, top, and bottom margins to deal with. Both aesthetic and practical considerations should be kept in mind when deciding on margins. Would you like to encourage your readers to save each issue of your newsletter? Leave an inside margin of at least three-quarters of an inch and punch three holes in it so that the reader can store the issues in a binder. Will your text benefit from sidebar notes in the margins? Then make sure your margins are wide enough for such items. Where will your running head go and how will it be designed? What kind of page numbering will you be using and where will it go? All these choices affect your margin size.

Don't cram text onto a page to save printing costs.

When choosing margin sizes, remember that *white space* is vital in a newsletter. *White space* is the space that is not covered with text or graphics; basically, it is the blank space. Don't think of white space as the unused portion of the page that is "left over" after you have covered as much area as possible with text or graphics. White space should be considered as part of your overall design. It is important to leave enough white space to balance the black areas of your page. A page crowded with text and graphics and with little white space is busy and daunting. White space makes your pages look calm, organized, uncluttered, and accessible.

Your goal is not to cram as much text onto a page as possible to save the cost of printing more pages. Your goal is to communicate, and white space is an important factor in good printed communications. So, if in doubt about the size of your margins, err on the side of generosity.

2. Number of columns

Next time you browse through a magazine, newsletter, or other publication, count the number of columns on a page. Most magazines have three columns, though two or four is not uncommon. Rarely do you see a one-column magazine.

Some newsletters do have one wide column; these are usually informally designed and often attempt to imitate the initimacy and immediacy of a letter. One wide column does not lend itself to much layout creativity and for this reason is too monotonous for more than a one- or two-page newsletter (see Sample #3).

Two columns is a frequent choice among newsletter designers. The two columns allow some layout freedom without requiring too much design with each issue. The wide columns permit the use of large illustrations (see Sample #4).

A three-column grid is the most popular layout for newsletters. The three columns provide great flexibility in layout. They also, however, require considerable skill in designing the pages for each issue (see Sample #5).

A four-column newsletter provides great challenge to the designer. With so many columns, the layout will have a tendency to become busy, with many different elements fighting for the reader's attention on each page. On an 8½" x 11" page, the extremely thin column widths can be irritating to the reader. On the flip side, four columns provide endless variability in design. The columns can be used separately or combined into two- or three-column illustrations or screened boxes. The three inside columns could be used for text and the outer one reserved for page folios, boxes, quotes, or sidebars (see Sample #6).

SAMPLE #3
ONE-COLUMN NEWSLETTER

One wide column does not lend itself to creativity.

SAMPLE #4
TWO-COLUMN NEWSLETTER

The two-column format permits the use of large illustrations.

SAMPLE #5
THREE-COLUMN NEWSLETTER

Three columns provide great flexibility in layout.

SAMPLE #6
FOUR-COLUMN NEWSLETTER

A four-column newsletter provides great challenge to the designer.

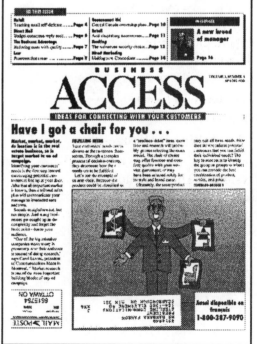

3. Column width

If you choose to make all your columns equal, the width will be tightly constrained by the page size and margin widths you choose. For example, a three-column format on an 8½" x 11" page with four-pica margins all around will dictate a column width of around 13 to 13½ picas. Your only area for adjustment is in the size of your "alleys," sometimes called gutters, the white areas between the columns.

However, there is no reason that you have to make your columns equal in width. All too often, newsletters are laid out with too much left and right balance. An alternative is to use an asymmetrical grid. A *Scholar's Margin Grid #1* (one narrow column and one wide column) or a *Scholar's Margin Grid #2* (one narrow column and two wider columns) help to create unusual patterns on a page (see Sample #7). The narrow outside column in each format is used for illustrations, callouts, subheads, etc. while the inner column(s) is used for the text.

Avoid column widths of more than 42 picas, as the eye has difficulty following the resulting long lines of text across the page.

4. Alley width

The alleys are the white areas between the columns of text. Your main consideration is to ensure that the alleys are neither too narrow, allowing the columns to run into each other, nor too wide, cutting off the aesthetic connection between the columns. Also take care that you are consistent in alley width — all columns and pages should have the same alleys. Alleys average between one and three picas in width.

5. Headers and footers

Headers are items that appear at the top of every page; footers appear at the bottom of every page. They include items such as folios (page numbers) and running heads (wording that, in newsletters, usually identifies the name of the publication). For your grid, you should decide what kind of headers and footers you want, where they will be placed (left, right, centered, in the margin), and their style.

Headers and footers should be easily found and easily read. Try to keep them short.

6. Putting it all together

Samples #8, #9, #10, and #11 show sample grids for an 8½" x 11" newsletter. These demonstrate how the various elements we have been discussing come together to create a standard grid that you can use for your pages from issue to issue. But, no matter how useful grids are, always remember that they are intended to be guidelines only, not barriers.

SAMPLE #7
SCHOLAR'S MARGIN GRIDS

Scholar's Margin
Grid #1

Scholar's Margin
Grid #2

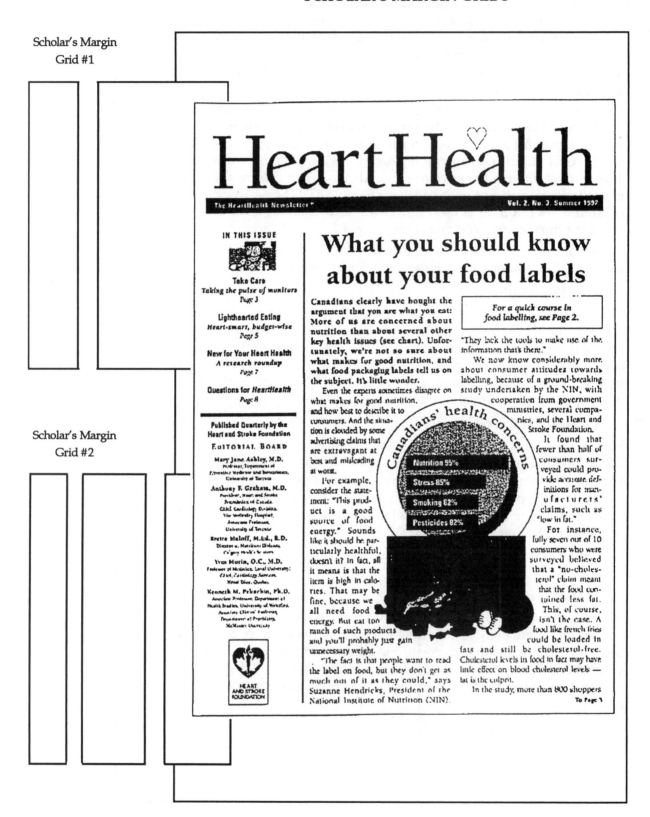

SAMPLE #8
TYPICAL ONE-COLUMN GRID

SAMPLE #9
TYPICAL TWO-COLUMN GRID

SAMPLE #10
TYPICAL THREE-COLUMN GRID

SAMPLE #11
TYPICAL FOUR-COLUMN GRID

c. *Other formatting elements*

1. Justification

Text can be *justified, flush left, flush right, ragged left, ragged right, or centered.*

Justified text aligns along both left and right sides. The computer creates justified text by adding tiny bits of space between the letters so that they fill out the lines. This is the most popular style of body text and, many argue, the easiest to read. This paragraph is justified.

Flush left text is aligned on the left side. *Ragged right* text is not aligned along the right side. This paragraph was typed flush left, ragged right. This is the second most popular style of text.

Flush right text is aligned on the right side. *Ragged left* text is not aligned along the left side. This paragraph is flush right, ragged left. Flush right, ragged left is rarely used in typesetting except in advertisements, cutlines, or callouts. This style of justification is very difficult to read, because the eye wants to return to the same spot after every line to start a new line. If the eye has to search for the beginning of the new line every time because it is in a new place, it slows down the reader considerably.

Centered text centers
the text in the column
or between the margins.
This paragraph is centered. This style is never
used for body text,
but it may be used
for headlines, flyers,
or inside a border.

Justified text is more serious and formal than ragged right, which has a more upbeat feeling. Ragged right has more white space, so it is a matter of taste.

Avoid justifying a column that has less than 60 characters per line as the result will be poor wordspacing and increased hyphenation.

You should decide whether your main body text will be justified or flush left/ragged right and whether that decision will also hold for special text, such as that inside frames or in sidebars.

You also need to consider your headlines and how you want them to look.

2. Hyphenation

To create justified text, the computer will usually break words with a hyphen at the end of a line if the whole word won't fit. The computer has preset rules about where to break words. What you have to decide is how many hyphenated line endings you will allow in a row (two or three are common choices) and where you want to overrule the computer's decisions. Sometimes, hyphenations are incorrect, and sometimes, they're unprofessional. For example, the computer may break an *already-hyphenated* word. In this example, you would have to "force" the "hy-" to the next line.

Many editors don't like this, so in situations like this editors may rewrite or cut text to correct the problem or ask the layout artist to adjust the spacing.

Headlines should never be hyphenated.

3. Widows and orphans

In typesetting jargon, a *widow* is a very short line at the end of a paragraph. Widows are also the first line of a paragraph when it occurs as the last line on a page or in a column. An *orphan* is the last line of a paragraph that appears at the top of a page or column. Both widows and orphans are undesirable because they create uneven rivers of white space between paragraphs. They also break up the neat rectangle that the text forms on the page.

Ideally, the last line of a paragraph should fill at least 20% of the measure, but this is often impractical. At least, a last line should be long enough to extend well past the paragraph indent in the line below it. Hyphenated widows — where the widow is composed of a word fragment — should be avoided.

For your format, decide what is the least number of lines from a paragraph you will allow at the top and bottom of a page. A good standard is that no column or page should begin with a paragraph fragment of less than two full lines or less than three lines if the last line is short, unless the text fills 75% of the line.

4. Paragraph style

Usually, newsletters use a paragraph indent. The size of the indent, which is usually one or two picas, depends on the width of a column. Avoid large indents since they make the page look uneven.

Indents help the reader see where a new paragraph begins. However, some modern styles eliminate indents, relying instead on additional space between paragraphs to signal a new paragraph to the reader. This is probably not a great idea for a newsletter that has a lot of text, as the indented paragraphs do make reading easier and provide white space within large blocks of text. Another choice is to indent all paragraphs except for the first ones under each heading, which is the style used in this book.

There are several other graphic ways of signalling a new paragraph to the reader, as the following sample sentences demonstrate. Whichever technique you choose, stick to one, and avoid mixing too many graphic elements.

(a) *Writing Concepts* **is a newsletter that uses a sans serif bold typeface for the first line of each paragraph.**

(b) OTHER newsletters begin a new paragraph with the first word or line in capital letters.

(c) Sometimes a hanging indent or overhanging paragraph is used for aligning lists or points of interest.

(d) • Bulleted copy is another way of indicating new thoughts.

d. Using graphics in your format

Graphics are visual elements such as stylized type, boxes, shadows, outsize caps, and screens. Some of these you will use differently in each issue you design. Some, however, should be set in place as permanent design features of your overall format. Sample #12 shows how graphic elements look within a newsletter format.

SAMPLE #12
GRAPHIC ELEMENTS WITHIN A NEWSLETTER FORMAT

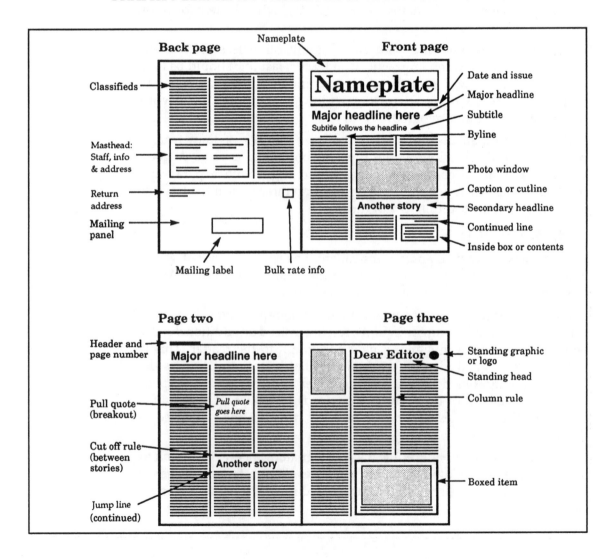

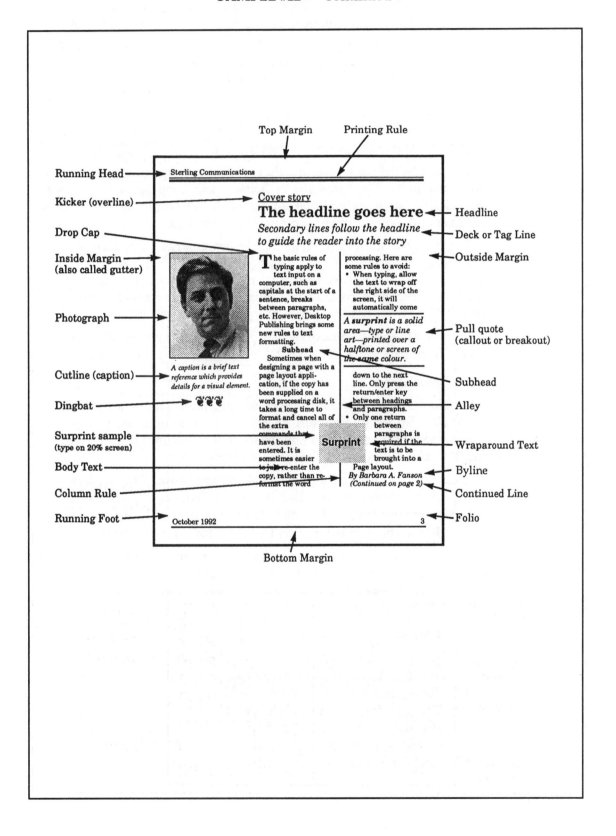

Top Margin

Printing Rule

Running Head

Sterling Communications

Kicker (overline)

Cover story

The headline goes here ← Headline

Secondary lines follow the headline to guide the reader into the story ← Deck or Tag Line

Drop Cap

Inside Margin (also called gutter)

Outside Margin

The basic rules of typing apply to text input on a computer, such as capitals at the start of a sentence, breaks between paragraphs, etc. However, Desktop Publishing brings some new rules to text formatting.

processing. Here are some rules to avoid:
• When typing, allow the text to wrap off the right side of the screen, it will automatically come

*A **surprint** is a solid area—type or line art—printed over a halftone or screen of the same colour.* ← Pull quote (callout or breakout)

Photograph

Subhead
Sometimes when designing a page with a page layout application, if the copy has been supplied on a word processing disk, it takes a long time to format and cancel all of the extra commands that have been entered. It is sometimes easier to just re-enter the copy, rather than re-format the word

down to the next line. Only press the return/enter key between headings and paragraphs. ← Subhead

• Only one return between paragraphs is required if the text is to be brought into a page layout. ← Alley

Surprint ← Wraparound Text

By Barbara A. Fanson ← Byline
(Continued on page 2) ← Continued Line

A caption is a brief text reference which provides details for a visual element.

Cutline (caption)

Dingbat

Surprint sample (type on 20% screen)

Body Text

Column Rule

Running Foot

October 1992

3 ← Folio

Bottom Margin

1. Nameplate

The *nameplate* is the logo or design on the front page that identifies the newsletter. It is also called a flag or banner. When designing a nameplate, you want it to be unique, simple, bold, clean, and reflect the image of your newsletter. Avoid busy or complex nameplates with too much type, logos, information, background, and graphic accents.

The nameplate must be large enough to attract attention, yet not overwhelm the front page. If your nameplate is too small, it will not attract attention; a large nameplate demonstrates a confident, strong graphic appearance. If you have the word *the* in your nameplate, you may wish to downplay it in size, since it is less important.

If possible, the nameplate should explain your purpose with a tagline: *Nuts and Bolts: The Newsletter of Boltfasteners Local No. 23.* However, subtitles or taglines should be smaller with less emphasis. The volume number and date should not compete with the logo.

Flexibility is important. Will the design enlarge or reduce without changing the legibility? Can you add a reverse, outline, shadow, or run it in two colors? Is it moveable to other positions on the front page? Make sure the nameplate is instantly distinguishable from the rest of the newsletter, especially from any headline that may appear immediately under it.

Sample #13 shows some of the various positions a nameplate may take on the front page.

2. Masthead

A *masthead* is a listing of contributors, writers, photographers, and editors. It should also include an address and telephone number, just in case someone wants to contact the publication. It sometimes includes a statement of editorial policy such as the following:

> Opinions expressed in this newsletter are those of the writers and do not necessarily reflect those of the editors or publishers. Readers are invited to submit their opinions in letters to the editor. Published letters may be edited for style or length.

Mastheads are commonly placed on the first, second, or last page of a newsletter. They are usually boxed or screened or set apart from regular text in some graphic way and thus become a continuing graphic element for your newsletter. Sample #14 shows some masthead styles.

3. Calendar

A calendar helps keep readers informed of upcoming events. While the content of the calendar changes every issue, the format and placement of it should always be the same so that readers can find it without effort. Your calendar's format will vary depending on how many events are usually included, how much detail on each item is needed, even how often the newsletter is published. Create a calendar style that expresses your newsletter's personality and that serves its needs.

Sample #15 shows some calendar styles.

Short story across the top

Nameplate

Main story goes here

Nameplate

Headline goes across the top

Short story

Nameplate

Headline across top

Short story

Main story goes here

Logo

Short story

Logo

Short story

Short story

When designing a nameplate, you want it to be unique, simple, bold, clean, and to reflect the image of your newsletter.

A masthead is a listing of contributors, writers, photographers, and editors.

NEWSLETTER TRENDS

A newsletter about newsletters
Vol.1 No. 2   Feb. 1993
ISSN 1183-1855
Newsletter Trends is published monthly by:
Sterling Communications
1920 Ellesmere Rd., Suite 104
Scarborough, Ont. M1H 2W7
Phone & Fax: (416) 261-0161

Publisher:
Barbara A. Fanson

Assistant Editor:
Brenda Ferrera

Contributors:
Jim Bannister, Debbie Davies

Photography:
Dave Kovacs

Subscriptions are available for $85 yearly (plus $5.95 GST).
© 1993 by Sterling Communications Inc.

This newsletter was created on a Macintosh IIvx computer with QuarkXPress, Microsoft Word, Adobe Illustrator, and Adobe Photoshop.

Newsletter Trends

Vol.3 No. 5   May 1993   ISSN 1183-1855
*Newsletter Trend*s is published monthly by:

Sterling Communications
1920 Ellesmere Rd., Suite 104
Scarborough, Ontario, Canada M1H 2W7
Phone & Fax: (416) 261-0161
Publisher: Barbara A. Fanson
Assistant Editor: Brenda Ferrera
Contributors: Jim Bannister
                        Debbie Davies
Photography: Dave Kovacs
Subscriptions are available for $85 yearly (plus $5.95 GST) 12 issues.
© 1993 by Sterling Communications Inc. Subscribers may reproduce any article, except "The Write Side of the Brain" providing they mention the name and date of our newsletter as their source.
Submissions are encouraged.

Vol.3 No. 5   May 1991   ISSN 1183-1855
*Newsletter Trend*s is published monthly:
Sterling Communications
1920 Ellesmere Rd., Suite 104
Scarborough, Ontario M1H 2W7
Phone & Fax: (416) 261-0161
Publisher: Barbara A. Fanson
Assistant Editor: Brenda Ferrera
Contributors: Jim Bannister
                        Debbie Davies
Photography: Dave Kovacs

Newsletter Trends

A newsletter about newsletters
Published monthly by
Sterling Communications Inc.
1920 Ellesmere Road, Suite 104
Scarborough, Ont. M1H 2W7
Phone & Fax (416) 261-0161
Editor: Barbara A. Fanson
© 1993 Sterling Communications

Calendar

February 14 & 22 **How to Write, Design
& Edit Newsletters**
seminars presented by Jim Bannister.
at the Radisson Hotel, Don Valley and
the Westin Harbour Castle, Toronto.
Fee: $295, group rates available.
Call 1-800-445-3443 for more info.

February 22 - 24 **Computer Fest '94** is an exhibition of
computers, software and accessories
with free seminars including desktop
publishing and designing a home office.
In the Arts & Crafts Building,
Exhibition Place, Toronto.

February 23 **Desktop Publishing by Design** is a
one-hour seminar presented at
Computer Fest '94. The presentation
begins at 11:30 a.m.

March 10 **Typography Seminar** presented by
Seneca College. Learn how to measure
type, recognize typefaces, and use type
like a pro to produce publications, sales
literature, and logos. For information,
call (416) 261-0161.

Upcoming Events

April 10 - 13
**Vicom 94/The
Electronic Design Show**
at the Metro Toronto
Convention Center.
Seminars of interest:
Understanding Print
Production and Newsletter
Design. For more info, call
(416) 660-2491.

April 27
The Newsletter Clinic
is a one-day workshop on
planning, writing, designing,
producing, and photography.
9 am to 4 pm at George
Brown College, St. James
Campus, Toronto.
Fee: $107, book: $25.
For information, call
(416) 261-0161

*A calendar helps
keep readers
informed of
upcoming
events.*

Monday	Tuesday	Wednesday	Thursday	Friday
Blood Donor Clinic in the cafeteria		Managers Seminar 10 am - 3 pm Rm. 216	Sales Rep. Meeting 4:30 pm Rm. 320	Turkey dinner in the cafeteria $6 per plate

Looking ahead

Losing weight is easier now with a
weekly dieters meeting in the
cafeteria every Friday at 12 noon.

Free word processing course for
employees is offered March 18 at the
College. To register, contact the
human relations office.

Sales reps will meet on Thursday at
4:30 pm in room 320.

4. Rules

Rules can serve several purposes including separating stories, guiding the reader, and adding a graphic element to an otherwise boring page. What you should be concerned about at this point are rules that you want to incorporate as part of your format. Vertical lines between your columns or horizontal ones at the top and bottom of your page fall into this category. If you go for the verticals between columns, restrict yourself to thin (one-half point or *hairline* rules) or thin dotted lines. Your horizontals could be more creative — doubles, triples, combinations of thick and thin, stacked rules of different lengths would all be acceptable in this context (see Sample #16).

SAMPLE #16
RULES

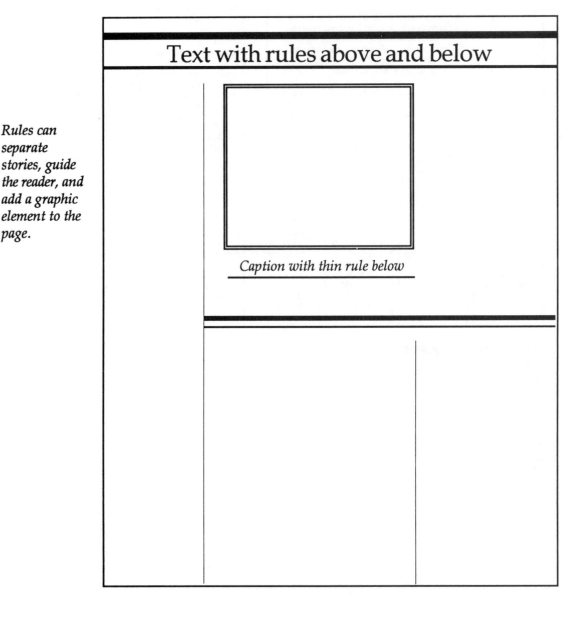

Text with rules above and below

Rules can separate stories, guide the reader, and add a graphic element to the page.

Caption with thin rule below

5. Refers

Refers are lines, paragraphs, or boxes that refer a reader to another page for information. Refers are used to cross-reference articles. Some refers will be boxed, others will be a simple line of type. Whatever style your publication uses, refers should —

(a) stand out typographically from the surrounding text. Refers often include rules, bullets, boldface, or italic type.

(b) be tightly written. Refers are signposts, so they should simply point not pontificate.

(c) be specific. All related items should have a refer that says more than "Other stories inside."

(d) be consistently positioned whenever used. Place them above the byline, at the top of a column, at the end of the story.

A refer line might look like this:

● How subscription newsletters are promoted, Page 5

6. Teasers

A refer is a signpost to guide readers to articles inside the publication. A *teaser* is more like a billboard. Refers advise; teasers advertise. They say "Open me: Hot story inside."

Supermarket tabloids are loaded with titillating teasers. Newsletters and newspapers have a more refined approach for their teasers (also called *promos, skylines,* or *boxcars*). Teasers are usually boxed in an eye-catching way at the top of the first page or stacked along the bottom. Most teasers combine a catchy headline phrase, a short copy blurb, and the story's page number or section. To be most effective, teasers should use art to gain attention.

7. Continuation lines and jump lines

When a story must be broken over two or more pages, the break and continuation on a later page are called a *jump. Continuation lines* tell you where a story is continued. They should be flush right at the bottom of an article. *Jump lines,* which indicate where a story "jumped" from are usually flush left at the top of the first column. Jump lines and continuations lines should be immediately distinguishable from regular text. You can use italics, bold type, a dingbat or some other graphic device to accomplish this. Each jump should have a key word or phrase that you then highlight in both the continuation line and the jump line. This helps readers find the jump on the new page.

8. Ideograms

Ideograms are emblems that can be used to symbolize the content or subhead of an article. Ideograms are a useful editorial tool. They help classify articles by subject and are especially helpful on pages with short news items or listings. They also add spots of color to a page.

Ideograms are simple graphics, helpful in classifying sections or columns of a newsletter.

9. Initial caps

Over-sized first letters add emphasis to the first sentence of an article. An over-sized capital letter may provide an important visual transition between the headline and body copy. An initial cap in the first paragraph also tells the reader to "start here."

Initial caps are an interesting way to add creativity and originality to your page design. A word of caution: avoid more than three initial caps per page. The term *initial cap* is often confused with a *drop cap*. An initial cap is when the first letter is larger than the other letters. A dropped cap is when the large letter is dropped below the baseline of the first line of type. Sometimes, the dropped cap will line up with the second, third, or fourth lines of type. Sample #17 shows different styles of initial caps.

10. Table of contents

Unless your newsletter runs to many pages, a table of contents is usually not necessary — readers can simply thumb through the few pages to find what interests them. However, whether or not you *need* a table of contents, you may *want* one.

SAMPLE #17

INITIAL CAPS

INITIAL CAPS

Initial caps are an interesting way to add creativity and originality to your page design. A word of caution: avoid more than three initial caps per page.

This is a raised cap. Notice how the baseline of the initial cap is the same as the first line of type. To create a raised cap, type the paragraph and then change the first character to a larger point size. Avoid auto leading, since the larger character will create more leading—space between lines of type.

This is a dropped cap—the first character is enlarged and the baseline is dropped below the baseline of the first line of type. Do not indent the paragraph. Sometimes, a dropped cap will line up with the second, third, or fourth lines of type.

An initial cap in a box is more creative and requires a page layout or graphics program. On a computer, it is quite easy to create, but since it is a separate graphic element, it does not flow with the text.

This initial cap has a horizontal scale of 50%. Sometimes, an initial cap can be placed in a margin.

Quite impressive isn't it? There are a variety of ways of making initial caps including drawing one in a drawing program and importing it into your layout. Click art is also available for initial caps.

Every initial cap in your newsletter should be consistent. How about trying a circle for variety? Add a screen or border to create the illusion of color.

See how creative you can be. Experiment with different objects, colors, and shapes. Obviously, a powerful graphics or page layout program will be needed.

Like a calendar, a table of contents is a graphic presentation of useful information for the reader. It is also a subtle advertisement of the newsletter's contents and serves to draw readers in.

If your table of contents is located in the same place and uses the same format every issue, readers will easily find it and the stories they are looking for.

11. Standing heads

Standing heads are also called column heads or logos. Their role is to identify columns and regular features. By using the same design and typeface for each standing head, you create continuity across the pages.

Standing heads may consist entirely of type and graphic elements like lines, or they may include a photo, usually of the columnist.

Sample #18 shows some standing head styles.

SAMPLE #18
STANDING HEADS

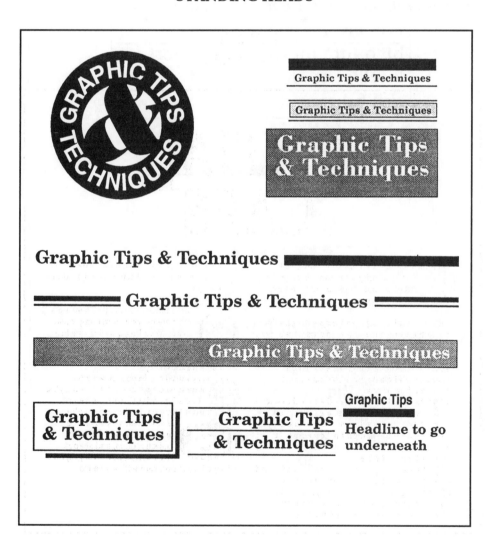

12. Pull quotes

Sometimes called *displayed quotes* or *quote outs*, a *pull quote* is a quotation or phrase taken from the text and displayed visually in special type. Sometimes it will be placed in a box, screened box, or surrounded by rules.

The pull quote should be an actual quote from the text and it should not identify the source — that would spoil the fun. The whole point is to get the reader's curiousity piqued so that he or she reads the article to find out who said it and in what context.

Sample #19 shows some pull quote styles.

SAMPLE #19
PULL QUOTES

"Quality is never an accident;
it is always the result of
high intention, sincere effort,
intelligent direction and
skillful execution."

Success is getting up
just one more time
than you fall down.

"*Free advice is usually
worth the price*"

"...the reason some people
don't recognize opportunity
is because it often comes
disguised as hard work."

e. Bilingual publications

There are several ways to format a publication with more than one language. The easiest method is to produce two separate publications. After all, if you combine two languages into one newsletter, people will read only half the publication. Bell Cellular publishes 700 English and 400 French copies of their internal newsletter *Domino*. The English version is written and designed using a computer. When the English version is complete, the translation is typeset over the English copy. Photographs and artwork are kept in the same locations. (See Sample #20 for an example of another bilingual newsletter.)

Quite often, two languages are combined into one publication because the cost of printing a 16-page newsletter is less than two eight-page newsletters. The most popular method of combining two languages is to place the second language on the back, upside down. Whether you're reading the English side or the second language, each of them is rightside up.

SAMPLE #20
BILINGUAL NEWSLETTER

Ford Canada publishes a six-page newsletter folded into three panels. The front three panels are English, the backs are French. The reader only sees one language at a time.

Another alternative is to have one language in the left column, and the second language in the right column. Unfortunately, the translated copy may not be exactly the same length. To even up the columns you could increase the leading (space between lines of type) of one language or make the column of the longer language slightly wider to accommodate the additional copy.

SIX SOURCES OF GRAPHICS

1. Dry transfer lettering or illustrations are graphics that you rub onto your page. Most stationery or art supply stores carry some brand of transfer film material including Letraset, Format, Chartpak, and Mecanorma.

2. A computer can be used for creating graphics by using dingbats or other characters to make a distinctive box or rule.

3. Clip art is available from companies such as Dynamic Graphics, Volk, or Dover. These line drawings are copyright free. An art supply store will probably have several categories of clip art books.

4. Click art is copyright-free artwork on a diskette for your computer. For names and addresses of click art, buy any computer or desktop publishing magazine.

5. Custom illustrations can be produced by an employee, member, friends, children, and art students in schools and colleges. Or, pay a graphic designer to illustrate your message.

6. Photograms are produced in a darkroom by placing objects onto a sheet of photographic paper and exposing it to light. The paper is developed and the result is high contrast art.

4
What you need to know about type

Good use of type is virtually invisible. Bad use of type is painfully visible. The reader may not be able to put a finger on the problem, but when he or she tosses aside the newsletter half-read because the body text gives him or her a headache, or misses important information because a headline was difficult to read, there is definitely a problem.

This chapter introduces you to type and its proper use.

a. *The terminology of typography*

To talk about type, you must know some of the special terminology of typography.

1. Serifs

Two terms that you will hear frequently when discussing typefaces are *serif* and *sans serif*. *Serifs* are the small, short strokes on the top and bottom of a printed letter (see Sample #21(a)). Obviously, serif typefaces have the serifs. *Sans* means *without,* so sans serif typefaces are "without serifs."

This is a serif typeface.

This is a sans serif typeface.

2. Leading or linespacing

Leading or linespacing is the space between lines of type. Leading (rhymes with bedding) is measured from the baseline of one line of type to the baseline of another (see Sample #21(b)). Normally, computer programs have *auto leading*, which automatically sets the leading to 120% of the point size of the text. If your type size is 10 points, the auto leading would be 12 points.

3. Kerning

When letters, such as "A" and "V" fall next to each other, they may appear to have an unproportionate amount of space between them (see Sample #21(c)). *Kerning* is the adjustment of space between two characters to make the word look better.

(a)

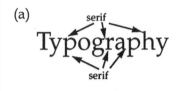

(e)

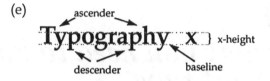

A baseline is the imaginary line that type rests on. X-height refers to the height of a lowercase x. an ascender extends above the x-height. A descender extends below the baseline.

(b)

24 point type
24 point type $\Big\}$ Leading

(c)

KNAVE   Not kerned

KNAVE   Kerned

The top example has not been kerned; the bottom example has been kerned to remove the extra space between characters.

(d)

7 point type
9 point type
10 point type
12 point type
14 point type
18 point type
24 point type
36 point type

Most newsletters use 9 to 12 point type for body text. Display type or headline type is 14 points or larger.

4. Type size

Printers and typesetters use points to measure type. This book is set in 11-point type. (See Sample #21(d) for other point size examples.)

5. Ascenders and descenders

The *x-height* of a face is the height of a lowercase "x." *Ascenders* are the parts of certain letters that "ascend" above the x-height. *Descenders* are the parts of certain letters that "descend" below the baseline (see Sample #21(e)). Type is measured from the tops of the ascenders to the bottom of the descenders.

6. Typeface

A *typeface* (sometimes called a *font*) is a set of characters with a specific design. This book is printed with Palatino typeface. Palatino has a certain set of specific design characteristics. These design characteristics are often too subtle for the non-typographer to note, but taken together, they give Palatino a unique look that would allow anyone to distinguish it at a glance from, say, Helvetica. Some common typefaces include —

Avant Garde

Bookman

New Century Schoolbook

Helvetica

Palatino

Times

Zapf Chancery

7. Type family

A *type family* is a complete collection of related variations and type styles, including light, book, bold, extra bold, ultra bold, oblique, italic, condensed, expanded, outlined, or shadowed. For example, ad designers who wanted to use Helvetica soon discovered a need for a thinner alphabet that still preserved the look of Helvetica but would allow them to fit more words in a line or simply to give a thinner, more sophisticated look. The result is Helvetica Narrow. Sometimes there are numerous gradations, providing faces with names like Demi Bold, Bold, Ultra Bold, and Black.

The variations may play upon the letters' thickness, their width, their slant, or other characteristics.

Typefaces that are thicker are said to have more *weight*. Thus, you might request a "heavier" or "lighter" face.

The following are a few of the many faces in the Helvetica family:

Helvetica Compressed

Helvetica Narrow

Helvetica Light Oblique

Helvetica Black

Helvetica Black Oblique

*A **typeface** is a set of characters that have an identifiable style, or design. A **font** is a complete character set of a particular typeface (e.g., Times Roman) in a specific point size. For example, the complete alphabet, both upper and lower case, the numeral set, and all grammatical symbols would be one font at 11 points, and a separate font at 12 points.*

8. Type style

Most text typefaces are normally *Roman* in style, meaning that the letters are upright rather than leaning. When words need to be emphasized or set apart in some way, they can be set in *italics*. The words *Roman* and *italics* are set in italics in this sentence.

9. Type groups

Type is classified into five groups:

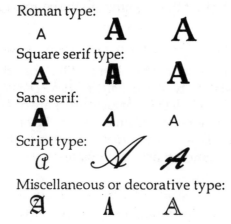

Roman type:

Square serif type:

Sans serif:

Script type:

Miscellaneous or decorative type:

10. Character set

A character set or font consists of all the characters in one size or one style of one face. (The word font is used two ways in desktop publishing, to mean character set and to mean typeface.) This sample shows all of the possible letters, numbers, and symbols that are available with 12-point New Century Schoolbook.

abcdefghijklmnopqrstuvwxyz

ABCDEFGHIJKLMNOPQRSTUVWXYZ

1234567890',./;'[]\=-~!@#$%^&*()_+|{}:"<>?""

b. Using type to enhance your message

1. The personalities of type

Every typeface has its own personality or look that makes it suitable for a particular type of publication. A typeface can project an image of confidence, elegance, boldness, casualness, novelty, romance, friendliness, stylishness, nostalgia, delicacy, modernity, or crispness — the possibilities are endless.

A particular typeface cannot change the meaning of the words, but it can enhance the message. The choice of typeface is particularly important when designing logos or standing heads because the image can be changed by simply substituting a typeface. The following are a few of the many personalities or moods that can be conveyed by typefaces.

(a) Trendy — Trendy represents fads or a popular look of the times. Avant Garde, for example, is a fashionable typeface that creates the impression of being on the leading edge. The characters are very round and refreshing. Modern, popular faces are trendy. Remember, however, that the trendy typeface of today is the tired or even nostalgic typeface of tomorrow. A typeface based on liquid crystal display (LCD) lettering may be the "hot-looking" face now, but in a few years it may appear as old-fashioned as "psychedelic" typefaces from the sixties do today.

(b) Nostalgic — Old typefaces that have earned our respect and remain popular remind us of the late 19th and early 20th centuries. Bodoni is a typical "nostalgic" typeface because it reflects that time period and is easily modified to create additional type styles.

(c) Traditional — Recognizable typefaces put the reader at ease. Readers see what they expect in the presentation of the material. For example, when reading an annual report, you expect to see traditional serif type. Bookman is a popular style that is acceptable in all situations and for all audiences.

(d) Classic — Typefaces such as Goudy and Caslon convey a quiet, natural balance. Their thick and thin strokes represent elegance in today's printed communications.

(e) Playful — Entertaining and light-hearted faces such as Frutiger have unusual contrasts of curves and straight shapes. A "playful" typeface will have contrast and an intuitive appearance.

(f) Aggressive — When you demand attention or a response, select a strong typeface such as Helvetica Condensed or Compressed. These styles create a sense of truth, importance, and urgency.

(g) Friendly — Type that is easy to read, appealing, and comfortable is "friendly." Optima is a typeface that combines the best characteristics of both sans serif and serif designs. "Friendly" faces convey feelings of warmth and personal communication.

(h) Flair — "Flair" in a typeface gives it a uniqueness. Many contemporary type styles, such as Zapf Chancery, have a sense of style and fashion. A typeface with an unusual letter or irregular angles may be distinctive.

(i) Informative — When you want to get right to the point, select a type that is informative and direct. Most textbooks and newsletters use a serif face such as Times Roman or New Century Schoolbook because they are not decorative and highly legible. Some sans serif typefaces can be for information.

(j) Sophisticated — Any typeface that implies a sense of beauty is considered "sophisticated." The characteristics include visual refinement of the characters and careful attention to conventional composition. Trump is a good example of sophistication in type.

2. To serif or not to serif

In body text, serif type is more readable than sans serif type:

This is 10-point Times, a common serif face and a common size. Notice how the serif text is easier to read than the sans serif text. Studies have shown serif type is the most readable, since the "little feet" help to guide the eye across a line of type.

This is 10-point Helvetica, a common sans serif face and a common size. Notice how the serif text is easier to read than the sans serif text. Studies have shown serif type is the most readable, since the "little feet" help to guide the eye across a line of type.

To improve the readability of sans serif type, increase the leading between lines of type.

This is 10-point Helvetica on a leading of 13 points. Notice how the extra leading improves readability. If you prefer sans serif type, add leading between lines.

Some newsletter designers choose a sans serif typeface, such as Helvetica for body text. This might work for newsletters that have little text, but is not recommended for most newsletters.

3. Choosing the right typeface

"There are only two kinds of typefaces: those you know how to use and those you don't."

There are hundreds of different typefaces, but that does not mean you should try to use all of them or even most of them in your newsletter! A designer for *Publish* magazine said, "There are only two kinds of typefaces: those you know how to use and those you don't." By using just a few faces, you can get to know them well: how to achieve contrast through different styles and spacing within the type family, which letter pairs require kerning, which typefaces "fill in" when reversed out of a black background.

Variety within a typeface is okay; but using a variety of different typefaces in the same publication can make it seem chaotic and badly designed. You should choose one typeface for your basic body text and perhaps one other or a variation on the first typeface for special uses such as boxed text, callouts, etc.

If you select a type that comes in a variety of weights, widths, and angles, such as bold, condensed, and oblique, you will have no trouble achieving enough variety to accommodate different uses.

If you choose a second typeface for special text, make sure that the two are different enough for the change to be noticeable, but not so different that they clash in style. For example, if your main text is a quiet, traditional serif face, don't choose a wild, ultra-modern sans serif face for your secondary text. Using a quiet, traditional sans serif face will probably be quite sufficient to distinguish your special text.

Currently, the seven most popular typefaces are Baskerville, Bodoni, Caslon, Times, Clarendon, Garamond, and Helvetica. Every Macintosh computer comes with Helvetica and Times typefaces, so they are being overused. *Overused* does not mean bad or wrong — just very ordinary. Perhaps *ordinary* is the look you need for your newsletter. Readers like familiar faces. What works in advertising — unusual or extreme typefaces — may not work for body copy or headlines. Some excellent serif typefaces for body copy are New Century Schoolbook because of its familiarity, Cheltenham because of its casual professionalism, and Garamond because of its classic elegance.

If you are using desktop publishing, your program will have come with a selection of typefaces. Many more typefaces are available for purchase through software packages.

Select a face that creates an appealing pattern on your page. Some typefaces appear darker than others, while others look too light or dark.

4. Choosing the right size

Once you know which typeface you want to use, choose a point size and column width that allows somewhere between 35 and 55 characters per line. Count all the letters, punctuation marks and spaces. Readability drops with fewer than 30 or more than 60 characters in a line.

Nine-point to 12-point type is an acceptable, legible size to use for body copy. Readership surveys indicate that readers prefer larger and more legible typefaces.

5. Headlines

Display type for headlines of newsletters should be 18 to 30 points in size. Headlines may have a different face than text, but you must still ensure that both faces are compatible. If you choose the same typeface for headlines as used for the body text, or a variation within the same type family, then you're safe because you know they're compatible.

6. Caps and lowercase

People have grown up reading books and magazines, so they are accustomed to reading lowercase letters. Words set in lowercase have a distinct silhouette that makes them recognizable, so people tend to "recognize" lowercase words rather than "read" them. Words set all in caps have no recognizable silhouette — they look all the same. Therefore, setting text in all caps reduces its readability.

IF THIS BLOCK OF TEXT WERE TO CONTINUE FOR ANY LENGTH, YOU WOULD SWIFTLY DISCOVER THAT ALL-CAP TEXT IS VERY DIFFICULT TO READ.

Avoid using all caps even for headlines. After all, your goal is ease of readability, so why make readers work even for the length of time it takes to read a headline? Studies show that type set in upper- and lowercase reads 13.4% faster than type set in all caps.

Since the headline is a statement, perhaps the first character should be capitalized, and the other letters lowercase.

7. Adding emphasis

Body text should always be set in Roman or plain type as this is much easier to read. If you want to add emphasis to a particular word or phrase, there are several ways of accomplishing this, but keep in mind two rules:

(a) Select the items to be emphasized and keep them to a minimum. Too many emphasized words, phrases, or sentences are confusing and they will compete for attention. It's like shouting all the time.

(b) Be consistent in your style. If italics are your choice, stick to italics, don't switch to boldface to emphasize something because you just used italics in the previous line.

Originally, <u>underlining</u> type on a typewriter gave emphasis to a word or thought. With typesetting, you can add emphasis with bold or italic type. If you choose to use underlining, the line can sit on the baseline and strike through the descenders. Breaking the line to leave space for descenders improves legibility. Placing the line below descenders will leave too much space between it and words without descenders.

Bold type is an excellent way of emphasizing a word, phrase, or sentence, but too many bold words can look very spotty and unattractive. Text set in all bold is very difficult to read.

Italic type shows a clear difference from the regular Roman text, but its weight may not necessarily stand out against the surrounding text. Text set all in italics is also difficult to read.

Although CAPITALS stand out clearly, they look unattractive if there are more than a few words. And, as discussed above, capital letters are more difficult to read, so keep them to a minimum.

Space can be used to emphasize a paragraph or quotation. An extra line of leading can be added before and after the paragraph to make it stand out.

You could also use a box, rules, or screens to set out certain lines or paragraphs.

In summary, all-caps is very dominant, italics are rather weak, and boldface makes a clear distinction.

8. Leading

In body text, use at least one point more leading than point size of type. For example, 10-point type on 11-point leading. If you have a long line measure or sans serif or bold type, increase space between lines.

Look at the x-height of the typeface. Typefaces with smaller x-heights can often be set more tightly than those with large x-heights.

Display type or headlines can be set more tightly. Display type (over 14 points in size) can be set with solid leading or leading less than the point size of the type. When using tight leading, avoid letting the ascenders of one line touch the descenders of the line above. (See Sample #21(e).)

c. Character modification: adjusting typefaces

Once you have selected a typeface, there are many things you can do to alter or modify it to fit your requirements. Most desktop publishing programs offer a variety of effects including scaling, tracking, outlining, and shadowing. By using these features you can change the look of your output.

1. Scaling and tracking

Scaling type stretches or squeezes each character to fit a word into a given space. This example shows Palatino with a width of 50%, 100%, and 150%.

SCALING

SCALING

SCALING

Tracking is the adjustment of spacing throughout a whole word or sentence. Tracking adds or decreases space between letters rather than distorting the letters themselves. This is Palatino with tracking of very tight, normal, and loose.

TRACKING

TRACKING

TRACKING

Some computer programs give variations of tracking such as no track, very loose, loose, normal, tight, and very tight. Others allow more precise control by adding or subtracting space in increments of 0.001 points.

In the past, typesetting companies handled the mechanics of tracking for designers. Because much of today's typography is composed by designers, it is important to understand how to mechanically adjust tracking for desired effects.

In most typesetting systems, the word and letterspacing is designed for the smaller character sizes such as 10 point. When the computer enlarges the letter to produce larger sizes of type, the letter- and wordspacing is also enlarged proportionally. As your letters get larger, you may need to reduce the space between letters and words to ensure aesthetics and legibility.

Try combining scaling and tracking to create a logo, display headline, or column head. Tracking has a major impact on the look of type. Remember, too, that it's nice to experiment, but extremes in either direction can reduce legibility.

2. Outlines and shadows

With a personal computer and a desktop publishing program, you can give a different look to the same font by making the letters outlined or shadowed.

Outline

Shadow

Outline and shadow work differently with every typeface; some faces don't work at all in these variations. Experiment to see how they affect your typeface.

d. Your type sheet

Now that you know more about type, you should be able to go ahead and make some choices. Your choices should become your standard style and should be recorded in a type sheet like the one provided as Worksheet #8. Use it to keep track of the typefaces, sizes, leading, and other specifications of your newsletter. By referring to the sheet over the coming issues, you will establish a recognizable, standard type style for your newsletter.

TEN TIPS FOR USING TYPE

1. If a page appears too dark, lighten it by increasing the amount of space between lines. Increased leading lightens the weight or color of type.

2. Avoid hyphens in headlines. Hyphens are acceptable in body text but display type (16 points or larger) should not be hyphenated.

3. Place more space above headlines than below. That way, the headline will "belong" to the article below it instead of "tagging along" with the one above it.

4. Use more leading on typefaces with long descenders.

5. If you use all-caps for something, be sure to visually space the letters after typesetting. The automatic spacing given to typefaces assumes lowercase letters, so all-caps words or phrases may need some adjustment.

6. Don't use a smaller point size to create a *small cap*. Proper small caps are designed by a typographer to maintain the typeface correctly as a small cap. "Home-made" small caps can't achieve this. Most computer layout programs include small caps.

7. Don't put space around em-dashes (the longer dashes used to punctuate sentences). A properly designed em-dash does not require extra space on each side (although you will see some publications that use the style of a space around em-dashes).

8. Do put spaces before and after ellipses.

9. Leave a thin space between a bullet and body text.

10. Make punctuation match the typeface or style of the word which precedes it.

WORKSHEET #8
TYPE SHEET

Function	Type style	Variation	Size	Placement	Leading	Lines
Article						
Headlines						
Subheads						
Kickers						
Banner						
Topic Heads						
Paragraph breaks						
Captions						
Bylines						
Margins						
Masthead						
Inside box						
Centerfold						
Boxes						
Calendar						
Page set-up						
Other						

5
Color

Why does red mean *stop?* Perhaps because it reminds us of FIRE or DANGER! Or because on a tree-lined street, red is easy to see against the green lawns and leaves.

Color is deeply rooted in human emotions. Color is used for several reasons: distinction, identification, designation of rank or status, symbolism, and direction.

Color can be used to create visual responses or generate feelings of calm, excitement, boldness, sadness, joy, masculinity, or femininity. Color can also be used to illustrate open and airy, light, or closed-in feelings. Various combinations of typography and color can bring vitality, interest, and variety to the printed message.

As designers, we have the capability of delivering messages in glorious color. But legibility and attractiveness must go hand in hand. If readers can't read it, you've failed. If they can read it, but won't, you're no better off. If your message is legible, but lost in the clutter of the competition, you still lose.

The *safe* way is to stick to black type on a white background. Safe, but boring. You likely want to use color, and use it effectively. You want to increase visibility and interest. It's up to you to select color combinations that are arresting, appealing, evocative, and effective.

a. Do you need color?

The first thing you should consider is whether your publication needs color at all and if so, how much color does it really need. Second, you must consider seriously whether your newsletter can afford full color.

Color may be wonderful, but if you are publishing a two-page stock market newsletter, you should ask yourself how much color is really going to add to the usefulness of the publication. Is color simply going to make your newsletter look frivolous? Is it going to add needless expense? Full color is very expensive.

Before adding color, make sure you are using black to its fullest potential. Adding areas of solid or screened black to an illustration, chart, or headline can give your page a variety of tonal qualities ranging from black to white. The range of screen percentages for one color gives numerous possibilities.

A screen of 60% black appears darker than 20% black, because the dots are bigger, but they are both produced with the same color ink.

Consider adding a screen bar behind a headline or illustration. Eye-catching drop-shadows are also very effective.

Try reversing art and type out of a large block of black for a special effect. Make certain that your type is large enough and will not fill in when reversed.

You can achieve various colors or shades of black by having gray heads.

Thick and thin rules can also create the same impression. Thick black rules are dark and add graphic appeal to a layout.

These are some of the ways you can give tonal variety to your publication without the cost of color.

b. Low-cost color

If you decide your newsletter could benefit from a touch of color, here are some low-cost ideas.

(a) Colored stock. The simplest and least expensive way to add color is by changing the color of your paper from white to a colored stock. Ivory, gray, or beige are popular, versatile choices.

(b) Colored ink. Another possibility is to change to a colored ink. Readers are so used to seeing black ink, a different color immediately catches their attention, even when it is used throughout the publication. When one color is used creatively, resourcefully and to its fullest potential, a one-color newsletter can look as good as expensive full-color jobs.

(c) Spot color. Spot color refers to the use of a second color on a page in selected spots. Typically, a spot color emphasizes a headline, logo, or boxes. Spot color is used when there is no need or budget for full-color printing.

(d) Preprinting a spot color. To save money, the nameplate, borders, rules, and other consistent items can be preprinted with the spot color on a year's supply of paper if the second color is always the same and always appears in the same place. You'll save money on each issue by preprinting and buying a larger amount of paper at bulk prices. The only drawback to preprinting is the lack of design opportunities.

c. Choosing an appropriate color

If you have a second color ink, should you use your corporate color, a different color, or change color with each issue? What the best color is for the second color is dependent upon many factors.

If the publication is a promotional tool for distribution to clients and prospects, using the corporate color is very important. Internal or subscription newsletters have the option of using the corporate color or changing color with each issue. Many subscription newsletters use the same second color to maintain continuity; readers recognize a publication by its color or identity.

Internal newsletters may benefit by changing the second color with each issue, since readers tend to differentiate issues by their color. Seasons and special events may suggest the choice of color — red in December, green in spring, orange in October, etc.

The frequency of your publication is an important factor. If your publication is weekly or biweekly, a different color each time is essential.

d. Full color through process printing

Process printing is an attempt to reproduce all the colors of the spectrum with just three colors — yellow (Y), magenta (M), and cyan (C) — plus black (K). By combining these inks it's possible to approximate almost any color. Color photographs and illustrations will normally use process colors for reproduction.

To separate the full-color image into yellow, magenta, and cyan, it is necessary to photograph the copy three times, through filters of the same color as the additive primaries: red, green, and blue. The addition of black ink improves shadow density and overall contrast.

Working with process color involves combining halftone screens to get the colors you want. On the printing press, each of the four colors is applied from a different printing plate. All four colors must line up exactly on the page. *In register* means that all colors match perfectly. Registration marks are used to line up the four pieces of film.

Each color separation halftone is made with the halftone screen placed at a different angle. When printed, the halftone dots are not actually superimposed over one another, but lie side by side, with a minimum of overprinting.

When printing in any color, the paper color, coating, and texture have an effect on the final printed product, as do the type of press and sequence of colors.

In desktop publishing, color separations can be done from your laser printer. Any item you changed to a color will come out of the laser printer on a separate sheet of paper. For example, if you produced a newsletter with black type and a red nameplate on page one, you would get two sheets of paper from your laser printer: one for the black ink and one for red. This way, you can check whether the color will appear in the right place.

If you are working on a computer with a color monitor, remember that the colors you see on your screen will be different from those on a printed sheet of paper. Colors on your monitor are lit from behind, which gives them a life and vitality they may not have when printed.

Are you able to change the ink color or paper color with every issue of your newsletter? Each issue could be an opportunity to experiment with color.

COLOR TIPS

- When choosing an ink color for a newsletter that may be copied on a photocopier, make sure you use a color that photocopies well.
- Be sure to specify the ink color by number.
- Get a sample of matching paper to see how the color looks over a large area.
- For maximum visibility, use colors that contrast.
- Ask the printer for good ink coverage.
- Look at colors that other publications use. See what works and what doesn't.
- Collect samples of ink colors you like in a folder.
- Give an older newsletter a new look by updating the ink colors.
- For regular publications, use the same spot color with every issue. Consider having the spot color printed in advance, then overprint the new issue.
- When selecting colors, always ask: Do I like it? Will the readers like it? Is it the best color for the piece?

Part 3
Content: informing and entertaining the reader

6
The editor's role

a. What does an editor do?

A newsletter editor wears many hats. Not only does he or she actually edit the written word, the editor also researches, writes, assigns stories to other writers, develops story ideas, chooses illustrations, coordinates staff, proofs, and coordinates the overall production of the publication.

The editor shapes the style and tone of the newsletter. This requires setting standards for readability, choosing styles for spelling and format, and ensuring that the content is accurate, consistent, appropriate for the audience, and of the highest quality possible.

In addition, since the advent of desktop publishing, the editor may also act as designer and layout artist.

1. Editorial advisory board

In many organizations and businesses an editorial advisory board assists the editor in setting standards for the publication, approving budgets, discussing upcoming articles and story formats, reviewing design, and providing opinion on controversial issues.

An advisory board is usually made up of a panel of unpaid volunteers. In a larger business, it may consist of representatives from different departments who can help ensure that the tone and style of the publication is representative of the corporation.

City College News is a monthly tabloid newspaper distributed to staff and students of George Brown College in Toronto. The newspaper's editorial advisory board meets once a month to discuss the upcoming issue and to review the previous issue. The board includes representatives of the full-time students, continuing education students, administrators, support staff, and professors. Each member of the board is a volunteer who donates about two hours of time each month.

b. Make your newsletter easy to read

1. Using a readability index

If readers must work hard to read your newsletter, they are not going to read it. It's as simple as that. So, one of your challenges as editor will be to make reading your newsletter as easy and pleasant as possible.

If your newsletter contains dozens of multisyllabic words that your readers have to look up in a dictionary, they are not going to bother. If the newsletter is peppered with inscrutable jargon inappropriate to the readers, it's not going to be read. If every sentence runs a paragraph in length, you're definitely going to lose your readers. These are all things that decrease the readability of your publication.

You can measure readability by using a *readability index*. This is a method of measuring approximately what level of education a reader needs to understand a particular piece of writing. The average reader reads at a grade seven level and daily newspapers generally edit their articles for a grade eight or nine level.

If you receive articles from a variety of sources, you should try to edit them to the same level of readability. You can check your success against a readability index.

One method is the Gunning Fog Index. Here is how to use it.

Step 1: Find a passage that has approximately 100 words in it and that ends with a period.

Step 2: Calculate the average sentence length by dividing 100 by the number of sentences in the selected passage.

Step 3: Count the number of words with three or more syllables. This number will give you the percentage of "hard words" in the passage. Do not count proper nouns, combinations of easy words like typewriter or newsletter, verbs that become three syllables by adding "es," "ing," or "ed" (e.g., caroling), or jargon familiar to your readers.

Step 4: Add the average sentence length (Step 2) to the number of hard words (Step 3).

Step 5: Multiply the total in Step 4 by 0.4.

The number you get as a result refers to the grade level of readability. Anything above 17 is difficult for college students.

Here is an example. Suppose you identify a 100-word passage with nine sentences in it. The number of hard words is eight. Divide 100 by nine to give you the average sentence length — in this case 11.1. Add the hard words: $11.1 + 8 = 19.1$. Then multiply by 0.4: 19.1×0.4 = a grade level of 7.64 (grades 7 to 8).

If the index indicates your average article is written to a very high level, you may want to edit it for accessibility, unless, of course, your audience expects a very high level of writing.

2. Edit for reading ease

You should always edit with the goal of making your newsletter easy to read. Every story that leaves your hand after editing should be clean, concise, and error-free. Try to improve sentence flow, expression, and technical construction. Fix all factual, grammatical, stylistic, or structural errors.

Ensure that the story is specific and interesting for the readers and opt for one interesting angle rather than a mish-mash of several styles or bases.

Move sentences or paragraphs to ensure that the story flows properly. If you must rewrite the lead to give proper emphasis or add color, do it. You can also move secondary information from the lead and place it lower.

Eliminate jargon and murky language. Be specific, direct, and vigorous. Long sentences can be broken into two if the sentence length seems to muddy the meaning. Make sure the article answers all pertinent questions and explains all unusual or technical terms.

Offer suggestions to the writer that are constructive, but not discouraging. Perhaps the piece needs quotations, color, or specific details. If you have to rewrite, strive to maintain the writer's flavor and choice of phrasing whenever possible.

See the list at the end of this chapter for hints on assigning articles to writers.

c. Working with contributors

Your contributors might include professional writers, amateur writers, and those who have never picked up a pen before. They may range from the president of the organization to an anonymous letter writer.

Whoever they are, treat them well. They are valuable to you. Contributors provide new perspectives, new voices, and fresh air to a publication. A contributor can make personal comments and take stands on issues that are inappropriate for the editor, who must try to reflect the views of all readers. Without contributors, you won't have much of a newsletter.

1. Make sure they know what you want

Treating contributors well means communicating with them so they know exactly what it is you want before you assign them a story. Make sure the writer understands the tone you want to take. Is it technical, personal, a feature, or a news item? Do you want a checklist, an opinion piece, or a detailed investigative report?

How long should the article be? A writer should know before starting the article how many words you expect. You don't want the writer to submit five times more copy than you can publish — that only creates more work for you and frustration for the writer.

You should specify whether you expect the writer to supply photographs, charts, drawings, or other graphics. You should also discuss what you will pay, if you are using professional freelance writers. When using contributors who are experts in their fields rather than professional writers who depend on freelance fees for their living, you may consider paying an honorarium of $100 to $200. For in-house experts, how about rewarding them with a certificate of appreciation or letter from the president?

And don't forget that affliction of all writers and editors: the deadline.

2. Editing humanely

If your editing philosophy is "Hand me the axe and to heck with the writer," you probably won't have to worry about contributors for long: you won't have any.

Most writers, particularly non-professionals, put themselves on the line when they write. They feel vulnerable and emotional about their writing, so be careful when you want to change their "perfect" words.

Editorial don'ts

- Don't rewrite extensively. Whenever possible, let the writer re-do it.

- Don't change copy unless you have a good, explainable reason.

- Don't overedit and make good writing mediocre.

- Don't do major rewrites merely because you would have written it differently.

- Don't shorten stories by cutting out human interest, important details, colorful explanations, or meaty quotations.

- If you do not understand the story, don't publish it.

Editorial do's

- If the article covers a controversy, do check that the writer has been fair to all sides. Remove material which could be libelous or in bad taste.

- If you're unsure, do check the reference.

- To build a good relationship with writers, do remember that you need to let them say no to your changes.

Editors tend to be perfectionists who focus on details, but they may get better results if they relax editorial standards and accept criticism as well as give it. The editor should realize that while it's important to have a style and stick to it, writers take their work very seriously and compromise may be necessary. If you feel your editor can't see the writer's side of things, let the editor write occasionally to find out what it's like to be edited.

Writers think of each article as a work of art. Since they have expressed themselves, they see their words as unchangeable. Editors need to appreciate what writers have gone through in facing and filling a blank page.

You can expect writers to be sensitive when they are writing in their own area of expertise. If you know the writer's specialty and background, you can guess what points may be touchy.

If the author prefers the original, avoid insisting on changes. When all is read and done, it's the author's piece; if he or she feels strongly about it, let it go. It's the author's name is on it, not yours.

When something isn't clear, write a query on a stick-on note. If the change is made, the author learns to be more clear. If you guess wrong, the author is grateful you didn't make the change.

Editors should avoid power trips. If you try to impose your own style on writers, it will never work. You can strive for perfection in yourself, but avoid putting that on others.

d. Style sheets

You need to decide how formal or "chatty" you want your articles to appear. An informal style of writing uses personal pronouns (e.g., I, me, we, you). It avoids jargon, but uses contractions and idiomatic English. Fragmented sentences are acceptable. Formal writing sticks to time-honored grammatical conventions and avoids personal pronouns and contractions.

e. Purpose of a style manual

All publications should have a writing style manual that describes acceptable rules for editors and writers. A manual should be clear, concise, and consistent. Most newsletter manuals are based on popular style manuals including *Canadian Press Stylebook*, *The Associated Press Stylebook and Libel Manual*, *The Chicago Manual of Style*, and the *New York Times Manual of Style and Usage*.

To develop guidelines for your newsletter, answer these basic questions:

- Who is your audience?

- Who will be using the style manual?

- Is it an international publication?

- Which style manual do you prefer?

A style manual is an essential editorial reference tool.

Sample #22 is a comparison of seven style manuals. When writing guidelines for your publication, here are 10 questions to consider:

(a) Serial commas — Do you put a comma before the and in a list of three or more?
Most newspaper stylebooks omit it.

(b) Numbers — What numbers do you spell out?
Most write out numbers from one to nine.

(c) Titles — Which ones do you capitalize?
Titles often take capitals before the person's name.

(d) Time — How do you give the time?
Associated Press says this way: 3:30 p.m.

(e) "Non" prefix — Is it hyphenated?
Most stylebooks do not hyphenate it, except the Associated Press.

(f) Compound modifiers — What requires a hyphen?
Most books hyphenate words like blue-green sea, well-known author, bluish-green dress.

(g) Decades — Spell out or use numbers?
Use an apostrophe with numbers? All accept numbers (some with and some without apostrophes).

(h) Possessives — What do you do with singular nouns ending in s?
Most style manuals add 's.

(i) Plural of letters — Do you use an apostrophe?
Most add an apostrophe (e.g., p's and I's).

(j) Movie or book titles — Do you use quotes or italics?
Two of the newspaper stylebooks use quotation marks, but the others prefer italics (e.g., "Gone With the Wind" or *Gone With the Wind*).

The style manuals compared in Sample #22 are among the most widely used. They should be available at your local bookseller or public library.

SAMPLE #22
COMPARISON OF STYLE MANUALS

		The Canadian Press	Editing Canadian English (FEAC)	Write Right! (Self-Counsel)
1.	**Serial Commas**	Tom, Dick and Harry	Tom, Dick and Harry or Tom, Dick, and Harry	Tom, Dick, and Harry
2.	**Numbers**	one through nine over 10, use the number 1 million citizens $2 million or $2,000,000	one through nine 10 three-room houses 1 million citizens $256 billion	one through nine 10 three-room houses 1 million citizens $256 billion
3.	**Job titles**	the president President Lincoln FBI Director Hoover company director Susan Smith	the president President Lincoln FBI Director Hoover company director Susan Smith	the president President Lincoln FBI Director Hoover company director Susan Smith
4.	**Time**	3:30 p.m. and 4 p.m. write noon, not 12 noon	3:30 AM in small caps a.m. and AM are acceptible	3:30 p.m. and 4 p.m. noon and midnight
5.	**Non**	non-aligned nation	non-aligned nation	non-aligned nation
6.	**Compound modifiers**	bluish-green suit full-time job well-known lecturer the dress, a bluish green works full time she is well-known	bluish-green suit full-time job well-known lecturer the dress, a bluish green works full time she is well-known	bluish-green suit full-time job well-known lecturer the dress, a bluish green works full time she is well-known
7.	**Decades**	1990s the '90s	1990s the '90s	1990s the '90s
8.	**Possessives**	hostess' seat Dickens's novel	hostess's invitation but hostess' seat is acceptable	hostess' seat Dickens's novel
9.	**Plural of letters**	p's and q's ABCs and IOUs	p's and q's ABCs and IOUs	p's and q's ABCs and IOUs
10.	**Movie titles**	*Gone With the Wind*	*Gone With the Wind*	*Gone With the Wind*

The Associated Press Stylebook	The Chicago Manual of Style	The New York Times Manual of Style	Webster's Standard American Style Manual
Tom, Dick and Harry	Tom, Dick, and Harry	Tom, Dick and Harry	Tom, Dick, and Harry
one through nine 10 three-room houses 1 million citizens $256 billion	one through ninety-nine ten three-room houses 1 million citizens $256 billion	one through nine 10 three-room houses 1 million citizens $256 billion	one through nine or one through ninety-nine 1 million citizens $2 billion; also two billion dollars
The president President Lincoln FBI Director Hoover company director Susan Smith	the president President Lincoln FBI Director Hoover company director Susan Smith	the President President Lincoln FBI Director Hoover company director Susan Smith	the president or President Lincoln FBI Director Hoover company director Susan Smith
3:30 p.m. and 4 p.m. noon and midnight	3:30 P.M. and 4:00 P.M. 12:00 noon and midnight	3:30 P.M. preferred to 3:30 o'clock; midnight	3:30 p.m. or P.M. twelve o'clock midnight
non-aligned nation	nonaligned nation	nonaligned nation	nonaligned nation
bluish-green suit full-time job well-known lecturer	bluish green suit full-time job well known lecturer	bluish-green suit full-time job well-known lecturer	bluish-green or bluish green suit well-known lecturer
the dress, a bluish green works full time she is well-known	blue green algae works full time she is well known	the dress, a bluish green works full time she is well known	the dress, a bluish green works full time she is well known
1990s the '90s	1990s the nineties	1990's	1990s or 1990's the '90s or the nineties
hostess's invitation but hostess' seat Dicken's novel	hostess' seat Dickens's novel	for goodness' sake Dickens's novel	hostess's invitation; also hostess' invitation Dickens' or Dicken's
p's and q's ABCs and IOUs	the three Rs, but p's ABCs and IOUs	p's and q's ABC's and IOU's	p's and q's ABCs and IOUs
"Gone with the Wind"	*Gone With the Wind*	"Gone With the Wind"	*Gone with the Wind*

f. Preparing a style manual

Here are a few procedures you may want to consider when establishing an in-house style guide:

- Analyze your needs. Who is your audience and how can you satisfy their needs?

- How much priority will the project have? Who will write the manual? How much time is available?

- Select a style manual. Several professional style manuals have been written; you may want to select one based on your audience.

- Determine the scope of your manual. How many pages are needed?

- Gather suggestions. Discuss the project with staff members and review past issues to determine which applications of the rules you are including.

- Present a draft. Review the project with editorial staff to discuss final decisions.

- Give a copy to some users for their suggestions. Don't go to press until you're satisfied with the input from various segments of your audience.

- Revise and print. The first run may be a limited number, since some manuals need to be updated or changed annually. Most publications fall somewhere in the middle.

g. ISSN (International standard serial number)

Most newsletters and other serial publications should obtain an international standard serial number (ISSN). The code identifies serial publications regardless of its language or country of origin. The number is unique, non-transferable, and internationally adopted.

An ISSN provides an efficient and economical method of communication between publishers and suppliers. The number can also be used in libraries and catalogues for identifying titles, ordering, and checking serials.

A "serial" is a publication issued in successive parts with the intention of continuing it indefinitely. Serial publications include newsletters, periodicals, newspapers, annuals (reports, yearbooks, directories, etc.), journals, memoirs, proceedings, transactions of societies, monographic series, and unnumbered series.

Each publication your organization produces that qualifies for an ISSN should have its own; two newsletters should have different ISSNs.

If possible, the ISSN should appear on the top right hand corner of the front page of your newsletter, though the back cover, title page or masthead are alternative choices. It is important to remember that if the title of the serial is changed, the ISSN must be changed as well.

h. *Legal deposit*

In Canada, Canadian publishers are required by law to send two copies of all periodicals published in Canada to the National Library of Canada. If your subscription rate is over $50, only one copy is necessary. The material is preserved in the library's permanent collection, where it is available for consultation and research, and most titles are also listed in *Canadiana*, the national bibliography. An official receipt will be issued when the copies are received. For additional information, write to:

National Library of Canada,
Canadiana Acquisitions Division and Legal Deposit Office
Ottawa, Ontario
K1A 0N4

In the United States, the Library of Congress has a similar program and requirements. For full information, write to:

Library of Congress
Washington, D.C.   20540

ASSIGNING ARTICLES

- The purpose of the piece
- The approximate length of the piece
- The nature of the target audience
- Sources of background material
- The time line for the piece
- When the first draft is due
- Who will be reviewing and editing the piece
- How the piece is to be handed in (typed, on disk; number of copies)
- How much time you expect the writer will put into it
- The amount and schedule of payments

If you have to assign a story to someone else, here is a list of things that should be discussed with the writer.

7
The inside story — developing content

People will read only what they are interested in.

Once you have set your objectives and have a firm idea of what you want to accomplish in your newsletter, you have to start thinking about the content. What features and articles will you include? Will there be regular contributors and columns? Is there essential information, such as a calendar of events, that must be included in each issue. And where will you go for ideas when the creative well runs dry?

a. The annual plan

Start by creating an annual editorial plan at the beginning of each publishing year. This is your chance to be creative — your opportunity to think about all the stories you would like to write and which stories you should write. This is also a good time to look at your audience. What are they interested in reading? Are there other people who work on the newsletter who would like to contribute articles on particular subjects?

For every subject area, write down several specific article ideas. Don't worry whether you'll offend someone — you can make changes later. As you go on, you'll find yourself getting more and more creative.

Don't forget to consider the business or political realities of your publication. Are there certain items that must be included in each issue — no questions asked? For example, many newsletters from businesses carry a message from the president. It may be expedient to do more profiles of senior management. Non-profit organizations, which have to be financially accountable to their members, might need to do a financial statement or summary once a year or more frequently.

If your publication is not new and you have back issues to refer to, draw up a list of all the topics you've covered in the past two years. As well, don't forget to look at your story bank to see what's awaiting publication. You may find that you've returned to one subject more often than you thought, or that you've neglected another for too long. Have there been more opinion columns than seem warranted? How long has it been since you ran a photo essay? This is the chance to plan the formats of your articles so that each issue is fresh and distinctive.

Pay attention to recent reader surveys if they exist. Again, find out what topics your readers want to see. If you have already written four articles on "holiday planning tips," for example, and your audience still wants more, think of a new way to present the information. Another format can bring new life to an old topic. Try, for example, a question and answer item with an authority in the field, or a photo essay rather than a news article.

Once you have a list of story and column ideas, rank them in order of importance. Arrange your lists in front of you on your desk. Now you can draw up your yearly editorial schedule.

Use a large sheet of graph paper or spreadsheet paper. Across the top, write down the issue numbers, dates, or months (e.g., spring, summer, fall, winter), and if you know in advance the number of pages available for editorial. Down the side, copy all the general subject areas from your lists, in order of importance. In the boxes where the rows and columns intersect, write *specific* article ideas. Make the rows and columns fairly wide so that you'll have enough space to write the information. You can use Worksheet #9 for this purpose, or adapt your own sheet.

In each square, write down a possible title for each article, a possible author, and perhaps even the format for the story — chart, checklist, question and answer, interview, profile, or expose. For example, if you put "Senior Management Profiles" under your topic column, you might plan to cover one person per issue and write their names under each issue column.

While working on the chart, pay attention to the mix of formats and ideas. Readers expect most of the information to be presented in expository essay style, so it's okay if two-thirds of every issue is in this format. Readers get tired of charts, photo essays, cartoons, and question-and-answer interviews if you overuse them. Readers also get tired of pronouncements from senior management, so try to balance them with lighter reading and human-interest stories.

At this point, you may have to file some story ideas to another time. Space is always limited, and keep in mind that a certain amount is used by required elements including the front page nameplate, masthead, and regular departments.

Now that you have your plan, you can make commitments. You can call a writer in January to book an article for August. Contributors and freelancers will welcome an assignment or commitment several months ahead of the deadline because it allows them to plan too. You can also make plans in advance to get illustrations and photographs. You can even plan a much-deserved vacation around your commitments.

b. Develop regular features

By including regular features in your newsletter, you can lessen the burden of coming up with completely new ideas and features for every issue. Regular columns can be valuable additions as long as you keep the three functions of a newsletter in mind: information, education, and promotion. Here are a few suggestions:

WORKSHEET #9
ANNUAL PLAN

Topics and Columns	Issue #_____	Issue #_____	Issue #_____

- Calendar of events — a listing of upcoming seminars, conferences, and classes may interest some readers. You can obtain data from other trade publications.

- Client of the month — profile a client benefiting from your product or service. Try to include interesting, progressive clients who will become faithful followers after being included.

- Interview — a 150- to 300-word interview with principals of your firm, prominent people in your industry, association executives, other publishers in your industry, key clients, staff, and other outside experts could be a very interesting feature article.

- Message from the president — a brief message could reflect the company's policies, forecasts, observations, personal opinions, or trends in the industry. Another branch or other managers could also contribute regular articles.

- Government regulations — important government legislation, new rules, or regulations and how they effect your industry will interest many employees or readers.

- Technical reports — articles on new equipment or technology will keep readers informed on developments in your industry. Include an assessment of the effectiveness, costs, and potential applications.

- Reprints and excerpts — if your company has a favorable review or article in another publication, ask for permission to reprint it. It demonstrates that your company is in the news! It's also a wonderful filler!

- Reports on seminars or training courses — attending an industry seminar or presentation can provide excellent material for your next newsletter, especially if you can obtain a quotation from one of the guest speakers or promoters. Best of all, most seminars have a show guide or course manual to assist in writing the story.

  Your newsletter may include details of training or night courses related to your industry. Perhaps the instructor will provide a quotation on a related topic. For example, if you hear a presentation on advertising, and you happen to be in the automobile industry, you could ask the speaker for a view on upcoming trends in advertising or on which method of promotion is best for automobiles.

c. Use fillers

When the material you slated for page three fails to materialize or is shorter than you expected, help is not far away. In the newsletter publishing business, it's inevitable that you will encounter a dry spell or run out of material just before deadline.

To keep your newsletter vibrant and fresh, keep a file of fillers that can be used for the last minute "holes." You can include copyright-free cartoons, community information, charitable events, sketches, photos, graphs, and charts. If you still need more, you might find it helpful to refer to the book, *Chase's Annual Events*. It lists offbeat and upbeat events, anniversaries, and birthdays for every day of the year. For example, April is celebrated as the International TWIT (tiresome wit) Award Month, National Humor Month, Month of the Young Child, Keep America Beautiful Month, National Woodworking Month, and National Anxiety Month (a good time to turn empty-page anxiety into productivity).

This book might inspire you to start a "Weird Facts of the Month" column or "Favorite Fact of the Month." Clip art can be tied in to demonstrate the column.

To order the book, send $32.45 U.S. to —
Chase's Annual Events
Contemporary Books, Inc.
Dept. C
180 N. Michigan Avenue
Chicago, Illinois 60601
Telephone: (312) 782-9343

d. Content ideas

As an editor, you want to make each issue interesting, both visually and by varying the writing styles of articles.

Test yourself. How many different writing styles and techniques have you used in the past year?

- 10 years ago — Look through your archives or previous issues for interesting trivia.

- Application articles — A customer expressing satisfaction about your product or service.

- Profile — Profile an employee, supplier, management, or association executive member.

- Interview — An important industry member or author to obtain their views on a particular subject.

- Tips or suggestions — Encourage readers to submit ideas on improvements in efficiency in their department or the organization.

- Industry pulse — News clippings of various related activities.

- Coming events — A listing of seminars, trade shows, or classes related to your industry.

- Product/company trivia — How does your company rank according to sales, number of personnel, etc.?

- Letting off steam — Encourage readers to submit their gripes or grievances.

- Opinions — Poll four or five members for their views on a specific topic.

- Press releases — Contact related associations, companies, and government offices to include you on their mailing list. Press releases could include new products, personnel changes, upcoming events, new books, or other related articles. And here's the best part — you keep readers abreast of the news but you don't have to write it!

e. Using feedback

Once you have published a few issues of your newsletter and have a plan for the coming year, you might feel in need of some assessment. Readership surveys can provide very helpful feedback and give you new ideas for future articles. Sample #23 shows a readership survey that you can adapt to your organization and newsletter.

Yearly readership surveys help maintain the focus of your publication by asking appropriate questions about the content. The most important ingredient of any publication is readers; without them, there wouldn't be a publication.

A penny for your thoughts...

Please give us your opinion. We'd like to know if you find this newsletter interesting and informative. With your input we can make it more valuable. This is an anonymous survey. **Do not sign your name.** *Thank you.*

1. Did you find the articles useful? ❏ yes ❏ no
2. Do you feel it is laid out well? ❏ yes ❏ no
3. Is it a useful newsletter? ❏ yes ❏ no
4. I would like to read about: _____

   _____

5. I would like to read more articles on:

   ❏ writing techniques ❏ editing styles ❏ editorial content
   ❏ design & layout ❏ graphics ❏ typography
   ❏ production ❏ desktop publishing ❏ prepress
   ❏ photography ❏ computers ❏ design makeover
   ❏ printing ❏ bindery ❏ distribution
   ❏ marketing ❏ promotion ❏ book reviews

6. Rank the following columns as

   1. Very interesting 2. Some interest 3. Slightly interesting 4. No interest

   _ the Write Side of the Brain _ Editing Newsletters
   _ Writing Newsletters _ Editorial Content
   _ Design for Desktop Publishing _ Promotion
   _ Photography _ Graphic Tips & Techniques
   _ The Printer's Report _ Distribution

7. Did you like the different newsletter design each month? ❏ yes ❏ no
8. Stories are generally: ❏ too long ❏ too short ❏ just right
9. Other comments or suggestions _____

   _____

   _____

   _____

GREAT IDEAS FOR YOUR NEWSLETTER

- Organization's plan
- Personnel policies and practices
- Productivity improvement
- Job-related information
- Job-advancement opportunities
- Effect of external events on my job
- Organization's competitive position
- News of other departments/divisions
- How my job fits into overall organization
- How organization uses its profits
- Organization's stand on current issues
- Personnel changes/promotions
- Financial results
- Advertising promotions/plans
- Stories about other employees
- Personal news (service anniversaries, etc.)
- Interview a new supervisor or employee
- How do demands of your work affect being a parent?
- Suggestion program
- Training or related educational opportunities
- Symptoms of stress in fellow workers
- New department or committee
- Define jargon in your industry
- Trends and management's position
- Are tours of your company available?
- How are we prepared for emergencies?
- What safety measures have been implemented?
- Has management introduced cost-saving measures for greater efficiency?
- A summary of annual reports
- What are our measures of quality control?

Have you ever sat at your desk staring at a blank piece of paper because you didn't know what to write? The next deadline is approaching and you think you've covered every imaginable topic. Here are ideas for articles when your creative well runs dry.

- How do employees spend time during breaks?
- Training programs for newcomers
- Explanation of payroll deductions
- Opinion column: print a question and three or four responses from employees, members
- "I remember when ...." Ask older members how things have changed and to share their memories
- Birthdays, retirements, obituaries, anniversaries
- Calendar of events, seminar, or trade shows
- Corporate donations and contributions
- Letters of thanks to employees from clients
- Questions and answers
- Changes in organization's policies
- Insurance benefits changes or additions
- Environmental/recycling programs
- Health and safety at your organization
- Classified ads (for members only)
- Application articles for external newsletters
- Testimonials from clients
- New products or services
- Current events and relation to your industry
- Healthy lunch alternatives to the brown bag
- New Year's resolutions (ask several employees)
- Positive stress (doctors' reports, books)
- Presentations and public speaking how-tos
- What will this company be like in 50 years?
- Unusual excuses or requests for anything
- The hazards of computer usage
- Understanding the annual report
- This newsletter is published for people like ... (picture of a reader with his or her name)
- "What is it?" contest
- Record, book, movie, or video reviews

- Counselling or therapy information
- Retirees: Where are they now?
- Lookalikes (Does anyone in the organization resemble a famous celebrity?)
- Telephone techniques
- Children's drawings of what their parents or grandparents do at work
- Courses at local schools
- Press clippings from newspapers or magazines of your organization or product
- "The customer who got away"
- "Did you know the computer could ..."
- Step-by-step explanations with illustrations

8
Good writing for great newsletters

Don't "preach" to your readers. Rather than selling management's view to employees or products to clients, a newsletter should educate the reader and stimulate a dialogue between the publication and its audience. Encourage readers to respond, either by writing, commenting, or asking questions. Write to express, not impress. Use simple words to communicate effectively; consider short sentences and paragraphs and avoid jargon.

To write appealing, readable articles, there are several writing formats that you can follow. By varying your writing styles, you can stimulate interest and add variety to your newsletter.

a. *Writing styles*

1. Inverted pyramid

The most popular method of writing is the inverted pyramid. Also called the five Ws, it is based on the five most important questions in journalism: who, what, why, when, where.

The essential information and facts are presented in the first paragraph or two of the article. This proven newswriting formula gives your readers the news quickly and easily. Less important information is at the end. If you have to cut words or paragraphs, cut from the bottom, where the less important information is found.

The lead paragraph answers the five Ws. The next couple of paragraphs provide important details, including How. You could add some more human interest, if you have the space, or you can provide less important details, some background information, or some history.

2. Profile à la *Wall Street Journal*

Another writing format used in journalism is copied from the *Wall Street Journal*. One large story is divided into three or four shorter stories. Sidebars tie the stories together. Each of the sidebars is a story with a headline.

Another interesting aspect of the *Wall Street Journal* profile is that an article may start with one person, describe the five Ws, and go back to one person. Usually based on one person's experience, the story may use human interest to sugarcoat the news.

3. The first person point of view

A less formal style of writing is based on your opinion or experience. This is especially effective for human interest stories.

For personal opinion articles, put the headline in quotation marks to add credibility. For example:

"In her own words"

4. Extended dialogue

To vary writing techniques, try an extended dialogue. Use quotes from several sources or interviews to develop a story.

An extended dialogue is usually chatty and informal; it's often used for human interest stories. Human interest stories have a lighter approach to reporting and they can be a refreshing change for your newsletter.

5. Question and answer

A solution to long, boring articles is the question and answer technique. The editor or writer prepares questions; the article provides the answers. (It also reminds the writer to stick to the point and not write any more than necessary.)

Usually the question is typed in boldface, while the reply is in regular face. You should double space before the question to visually separate the various items.

Almost any topic can be covered with this method.

Q: *What is an interesting method of presenting an article?*

A: *The question and answer technique.*

6. Interviews

Personal opinions always make a piece more interesting. Interviewing several people will make your article more credible. Interviews can be conducted among experts and among the newsletter readers themselves.

Readers like interviews because they add variety. A conversation between the writer and the person being interviewed is another informal way to share information.

In interviewing, the answers are everything. To start, you just need a few questions. Once you have some good meaty answers, you can edit the questions later. A good question is a dumb question. Avoid asking questions that can be answered by yes or no. Open-ended questions begin with Who, What, When, Where, Why and How. Or they could start with "Tell me about ..." or "Could you describe... " or "Would you explain...."

Use a tape recorder. Explain to the interviewee, "Rather than rely on my memory or notes, let me use this to get it right." Then place a small Walkman-sized cassette recorder with a built-in mike on the desk and discuss other topics such as the weather or sports. After a while, the interviewee will forget it's there.

Another reason for using a tape recorder is to protect yourself from being accused of misquoting someone. You will always have the truth on tape to settle disagreements.

Let the interviewee help you edit. Promise to show him or her the article before you have it typeset. The interviewee has the comfort of feeling in control and you get help with rewriting and editing.

7. Testimonials

Testimonials can be very effective. Nationally known figures, local authorities, experts, or just "plain folks" can be very convincing when they are sincerely behind a service or product. My computer retailer publishes a quarterly newsletter that features a customer on the front cover. The article describes how and why a computer is used. One issue featured Olympic skier Steve Podborski because he uses a Macintosh computer.

8. A quiz

Can you name 10 methods of keeping your newsletter interesting?

Readers find it difficult to ignore a quiz, especially when answers give them information about themselves. Any article that starts with "Test your knowledge of ..." is likely to draw readers. For example, a municipal energy group might start a story with "Can you name five ways to keep your house warmer this winter?" Multiple choice answers make tests easier to take.

9. Practical tips

Another method of adding interest is to offer tips that relate to your subject. "Five ways to..." could introduce an article of useful tips and advice on your subject.

An article on how to quit smoking might boil down the information to key tips, which are organized to reflect the quitting process.

10. More articles, fewer columns

To create a more interesting newsletter, try to have more articles than columns. Regular columns can be vague, written by office personnel, and topped by dull headlines such as "President's Report" or "Training Committee Report." Most readers won't bother to read them.

Important information could be lost in that boring "President's Report." Rather than write one long column, write several shorter articles with inviting headlines. The president could write the article, or you could quote the president in an article or interview. Add a headline that offers a benefit to readers, so they will be eager to read it. If there's nothing going on, leave it out to save the readers' time.

11. How-to information

Appropriately written how-to articles can provide valuable technical knowledge and practical experience. For example, you may discuss union grievance procedures, people's legal or contract rights, what child-care services are available, computer shortcuts, how to repair something, or how to reduce, reuse, or recycle garbage.

A word of caution: translate technical jargon into everyday language. Don't forget to discuss the readers' benefits — don't just explain how to do something, but explain how they can use it.

If you're writing about government cutbacks or local strikes, perhaps you can mention some alternatives.

12. Personal experiences

Real-life examples can provide ideas for articles, as well as add interest. A repair technician could write a story about a unique encounter during his routine schedule. Perhaps he saved an elderly person who had fallen down the stairs hours before he arrived.

Not only are human interest stories exciting, but they encourage other members to contribute articles. And that means less writing for you!

When reporting layoffs, you could include an interview about how a department is struggling with fewer staff. You could add human interest by interviewing a laid off employee.

All members have a story or minor success to share. Encourage readers to submit articles on real-life experiences.

13. Exposes

Wouldn't it be great to uncover some wrongdoing? When you expose behind-the-scenes maneuvers and get to the root of a crisis, your publication becomes an important vehicle.

If you develop a reputation for exposing and getting action on injustice, whistle-blowers will call you first with juicy information. When I was the editor of my college newspaper, I reported that the student president was using the student council's van to go to bars; it was the most well-read story that year. Although they threatened to fire me, or censor the newspaper, they couldn't deny it. The front page photo showed the van in front of a bar.

14. Analysis

People like statistics, charts, graphs, and analysis of local conditions. Readers will understand current issues better if explained in everyday language. Why is management cutting back on pay increases? Why do businesses need regulations? What can the reader do to help?

Explain your groups' principles and opinions. What associations do they advocate or support?

15. Point form

The point form style of newsletter writing lets you present a lot of information clearly, powerfully, and above all briefly. Point form is a series of simple sentences, sentence fragments, phrases, or even single words, to communicate facts.

This style of writing was exclusive to newsletters and bulletins, but now newspapers and magazines have adopted the style. Even some books written in the 1990s are no more than collections of lists. Point form is appropriate for —

- a collection of facts

- a chronology or history

- a summary of facts

- a brief of a report or other lengthy document

- an argument, the presentation of "reasons why"

- "how-to" articles or step-by-step instructions.

Readers love point form. People just don't have time to wade through long paragraphs. Using one or more lists in a story gives them an easy-to-read alternative.

Here are some do's and don'ts to observe:

- DO keep points brief, one or two lines tops.

- DON'T worry about using complete sentences. Sentence fragments are fine.

- DON'T number the points. Readers like to establish their own priorities.

- DO use bullets and dingbats to indicate the points.

Lists can be used within a story to break up long passages. Or, if you want a message to stand out in your reader's mind, you can use them outside the story by creating a sidebar with points. The sidebar summarizes the article. All the facts are in the lengthy version for those who have the time to read in detail. Let your article raise a point or two!

16. The great debate

Everyone has an opinion these days! Enter the great debate. Get two writers to put their opposing thoughts on the same subject in articles of equal length. Editors should not debate with their writers, so if you have one credibly biased submission, get another contributor to write the contrary view.

The editor must organize the copy to make sure contributors are addressing the same points in the same order, so the two columns combined truly resemble a debate. Use the question and answer format, giving them four or five questions to answer.

The best layout for a written debate is a two-column grid, with the opposing views running side-by-side. Running one on the top half of the page and the other on the bottom suggests you prefer the top one; don't do it.

Another attention-getter could be photos or illustrations of the writers, one in the left margin and one in the right, glaring at each other across the page.

Make sure you give it a good headline. "The Great Debate" is not enough, because it doesn't say what the debate is about. But you can use it as a kicker.

b. Encourage reader participation

Encourage readers to contribute stories or experiences that were embarrassing or outrageous. If the nature of the article permits, you can also include a photograph of the writer.

Not only are you encouraging reader support, but it's one article you don't have to write!

c. Quotations

One of the things that distinguishes newsletter writing from traditional journalism is the first-person format. Such a story requires a first person headline, like "They laughed when I sat down at the piano." And that headline should be in quotation marks. It's not the "I" that attracts the reader; it's the quotation marks!

Using a quote as the first sentence of your lead-in paragraph is another time-honored device. It's like a preacher announcing the text at the beginning of a sermon. It gets attention and sets the theme for the article. Don't simply repeat the quote you used in the headline. Find a quote that expands or reinforces the headline, or explains it — or even contradicts it — the more outrageous the better! The same technique can be used to close a story. You can devise a quote that summarizes the point of the article or calls the reader to action.

Quotations may be introduced into the text in two ways:

(a) run in, starting in the same line as the text and enclosed in quotation marks; or

(b) set off, starting one line beneath the text, without quotation marks.

Block quotations are usually indented from the left.

See chapter 12, section e. for the legal considerations of using quotations.

d. Features to avoid

Does your newsletter contain continuing features or standing columns such as —

- history of the organization

- minutes of the annual meeting

- honors and awards

- recipes and household hints

- puzzles, contests, and jokes

- message from the president

These columns are boring. Some of them, like recipes, contests, and humor columns, are mildly interesting as a diversion, but they are useless.

Distribute a readership survey. See which items get the lowest "read regularly" scores. The president's message will be near the top of the list, with the others following closely behind.

e. Story endings

The lead is vital, for it captures the reader, but the greatest point of emphasis in the story is the ending. We remember what we read last; that final hilarious anecdote, searing quote, startling fact, memorable scene, or succinct summary is what we remember from the story.

The traditional news story used to start strong and trail off. A story finished with the least important information so that a story could be cut from the bottom. Remember the inverted pyramid? Readers of newsletters demand a sense of completion: stories that come to a conclusion.

Some writers write the ending first. They have to know where they're going to decide how to get there.

Good endings are not summaries or conclusions. Good endings are not devices or fancy phrases. Good endings, like leads, are constructed of information that matters to the reader.

Writers should write strong endings that tell the reader as much as they show the reader. End with a quotation. A quotation is a piece of information, but its credibility comes from the speaker, not the writer. It provides a sense of objectivity to the story, and it allows for a conclusion in a way that readers will accept and believe. Or, you can end with an anecdote, which is a brief story combining character, place, dialogue, action, and reaction. It summarizes by implication and demonstration.

f. Writing guidelines

Here are some guidelines that should be observed when writing articles for newsletters or other communication projects.

1. Consider your audience

Write your material to be appropriate for your audience.

Write to the audience. This is the most important rule. The message you are trying to convey to the reader must be suited to the reader's needs in terms of content, style, language (level of difficulty), and layout. You should also consider your audience when you —

- organize your material. Plan your message so that readers can follow your meaning. Include plenty of headings or captions, so the reader does not have to consume large amounts of data to get a single fact.

- rewrite, revise, and edit your material. Aim for clarity, simplicity, continuity, and brevity.

- use charts and artwork to illustrate your message. "A picture is worth a thousand words" so include graphs, illustrations, tables, maps, and diagrams to break up the printed page. These help the reader to visualize the point, and they relieve the eye and brain strain of page after page of written material.

2. Know your subject

The first step to knowing your subject is knowing your objectives. Once you know what an article should achieve, eliminate all the things that do not advance your goal. For instance, you'll want to —

- use clear, short, familiar words. When you use unfamiliar words, your readers will read around the word and may misinterpret what you've written. If a reader has to look up the meaning of a word in a dictionary, he or she will be upset by the inconvenience. Avoid using a long word when a short one will do.

- eliminate unnecessary words. Overly descriptive words such as adjectives and adverbs may not be required if they obscure meanings.

- keep sentences short and simple. Long sentences increase resistance between the writer and the reader and impair communication. The average sentence in newsletter writing is between 10 and 15 words. Long sentences may confuse the reader. In addition, as a sentence becomes longer, the chance of making a grammatical error increases dramatically.

- use the active voice. Sentences are natural and straightforward when you use active voice, such as "The editor used a computer." If you change the sentence into the passive voice, the subject and direct object are switched: "A computer was used by the editor." The word editor was a subject but now it is an indirect object of the preposition "by" in the passive voice, and the sentence is less direct — less "active." Sometimes prepositional phrases are dropped because they aren't absolutely necessary. "A computer was used."

- use the imperative mood occasionally. In the imperative mood, the subject of the sentence is understood to be the second person pronoun "you," so it is left out. "Write to your local association for more information" is an example.

- use point form. When you need to list three or more items, consider using point form rather than separating the items by commas or semicolons. This also increases the amount of white space on the page, which reduces eye and brain strain. Numbers and letters should be used for sequential items, and dashes or bullets should be used for nonsequential items.

3. Adapt your style to fit your audience

Use language, grammar, and punctuation pragmatically, not literally. Do not be strictly bound by rules. Rules were meant to be broken, or stretched. If necessary, you may —

- begin sentences with "and" or "but"

- end sentences with prepositions

- use the same terms consistently (the reader may be confused if you change words)

- decrease the amount of punctuation which would be grammatically correct.

Use a conversational style. Write a story as you would verbally tell it. That doesn't mean you should use slang, just that you should be informal, rather than formal. Most people communicate better when they are speaking than when they are writing. Pretend you're talking to another person when you're writing. Put yourself in the speaking mode, rather than in the writing mode.

4. Use constructions that make the meaning clear

Keep construction parallel. Parallel construction means that parts of a sentence that are parallel in meaning should be parallel in structure. Don't write, "She likes swimming, running, and to play the piano." Instead, make the activities parallel by writing, "She likes swimming, running, and playing the piano."

Allow meaning to determine whether collective nouns are plural or singular. "The Board is pleased to announce the promotion of Jane Doe to managing editor." The Board is acting together as a single unit, and the singular form is used. Here's an example of a plural collective noun: "The Board were split in their views of the new style manual."

Use positive words rather than negative words. Some words evoke a positive or negative response. Which example do you prefer?

Turn off the computer when you leave.

or

Don't neglect to turn off the computer when you leave.

Use transitional words to smooth relationships between ideas, sentences, and paragraphs. Avoid abrupt changes when you shift from one topic to another or from one paragraph to another. Adopt the following transitional words: accordingly, presumably, although, however, since.

5. Grammar and usage

Pay heed to proper word usage. Words can have *similar*, but not *equivalent* meanings. A good writer strives to use the best word possible. Here are some examples of words that are often misused:

- *Fewer* refers to number, but *less* modifies a singular noun.

- *Anxious* means worried; *eager* means desirous.

- *Disinterested* means without self-interest; *uninterested* means not interested.

- *Almost* means nearly; *most* is the superlative form of much.

- *Numerous* refers to an exact but unknown number, and *many* is a large, indefinite number.

Ensure subject and verb agreement. The words linked to the subject and the verb do not always affect the number of the verb. For example: "Jane, as well as other members, was a good writer." It is incorrect to say: "Jane, as well as other members, were good writers." Some singular nouns that may cause confusion are: each, everybody, everyone, anyone, no one, nobody, anybody, etc. Check a grammar reference book if you are unsure.

6. Final checking

It's a good idea to have a fellow writer "idiot-proof" your written work before you distribute it. This will ensure that you have clearly expressed yourself, especially if the person doing the checking knows nothing about the subject matter. Computer spell checkers and grammar checkers are also helpful, but they won't catch the content or fact errors that a careful reader will.

g. Biased writing

Biased writing contains remarks about a person's sex, race, religion, age, or physical appearance that are not pertinent or demean or classify that person unnecessarily. Biased writing is evidence of an author who is either unaware, insensitive, or lazy.

Here are a few guidelines for recovering from biased writing:

- Use titles equally. Don't say "Mrs. John Jones and Cheryl Trane."

- Occupations and characterizations should be neutral. Don't refer to nurses as "she" and doctors as "he" or call every executive "he" and every secretary "she."

- Ask yourself if a descriptive phrase is really necessary to the story. Why point out the new sales representative is black? Would you point out that a sales representative is white?

An easy way to eliminate gender bias is to recast the sentence in the plural. Instead of saying "Each employee should log off his computer before leaving," say "Employees should log off their computers before leaving."

Another possibility is to delete the personal pronoun. For example, "A singer must practice his songs all the time" can be changed to "a singer must practice songs all the time." In these examples, a definite or indefinite article or another noun replaced the personal pronoun:

- "If an employee is late, notify his immediate supervisor" becomes "If an employee is late, notify the immediate supervisor."

- "Ask your teacher about report cards. He will inform you" can be changed to "Ask your teacher about report cards. The teacher will inform you."

You can also rewrite the sentence and use the second person "you" as the subject: "Ask your teacher to inform you about report cards." Sometimes rewriting the sentence to use the first person (I, me, mine) is the solution. For example, change "what are his rights" to "what are my rights?"

Avoid using he/she and his/her. The slashes interfere with smooth reading.

Here are some non-sexist alternatives for words that are gender exclusive:

(a) man: human race

(b) man on the street: average person

(c) manpower: workforce, personnel, staff

(d) chairman: chair

(e) spokesman: speaker, representative

(f) policeman: police officer

(g) stewardess: flight attendant

(h) salesman: sales representative

(i) housewife: housekeeper, homemaker

Try to avoid using awkward constructions such as *chairperson* or *spokesperson,* unless that is the person's title.

h. Increase the appeal of an article

Any topic can be made more interesting. Here are some methods for making your writing more captivating:

1. A startling fact

Begin with surprising information to engage your reader. Numbers make startling facts even more dramatic. For instance, you could begin an article with "Eighty percent more newsletters are being produced today than ten years ago." Look for startling or dramatic data related to your subject.

2. An intriguing question

Another technique is to begin with a question that catches the interest of your reader. For example, if you were writing an article about senior citizens, a major concern is being able to continue to drive. You might start a piece with "Will this man pass his driving test?" A photo of an elderly person would catch the interest of readers.

3. A common myth

What are the most commonly held myths that relate to the subject? They can make an excellent introduction. A few examples include: "They say Americans are the most fit people on the earth. But four out of five are overweight." Or "Starches are fattening: True or False?" This method may be effective for subjects that have many misconceptions.

4. Interesting anecdotes

A good way to involve a reader is to start with someone's personal story. "Driving in New York City is always an adventure. The last time Michelle..." Most of us find a good anecdote seductive. Collect ones that relate to your subject for your publications.

5. New information

New information attracts attention. Even using the word "new" seems to make information more appealing. You may as well take advantage of it if you have something new to say. An article about restaurants may start with the newest trends in eating out, or the most popular food among restaurants. There is always something new in every subject, and anything "new" is news.

6. A slice-of-life

The success of *People* magazine and the *National Enquirer* suggests we have an interest in other people's lives. Begin your story with a "slice-of-life." Common people and everyday situations that readers can relate to have a broad appeal. No matter what the topic, there is a way to relate it to some human experience. If you're writing about car phones, you might begin with: "Every week Erin spends Monday through Friday driving from Kitchener to Toronto."

7. Interesting comparisons

Another way to make your writing more appealing is to use interesting comparisons. If you are writing about difficult information, they can be especially useful. If you were trying to convince people about the safety of air travel, you could compare the odds of getting hurt while flying with those of riding in a car. You could also compare this year's product with last year's. People are also interested in numbers, rankings, and comparisons. Twenty years ago my favorite magazine cost 35¢. It now costs $4.95.

TEN TIPS TO COMBAT WRITER'S BLOCK

Even people with the most important things in the world to say find it difficult to get started. It's sad to see a writer with good ideas produce a poor article because the person spent too much time on the introduction.

Here are some rules to help you get your article off the ground.

1. Scribble down a tentative introduction simply to get yourself writing. You can change it later, since you don't know yet how the article will develop. If you're writing a feature article, consider leaving the first few lines blank, and write the introduction after you've written the story.

2. Start at the end. If you can't think of a leading paragraph, how about a closing paragraph?

3. Write down all the facts and information you need to know to write the story. If you can shake a few ideas lose, you may realize how to approach the story or the angle to take. Use one of the facts as the lead.

4. Think of an analogy or metaphor.

5. List 10 frequently asked questions about the subject. Not every story has to be a creative masterpiece. The question and answer story format is a reader favorite. Keep the questions simple and the answers brief. This exercise forces you to write tightly.

6. Writer's block may be caused by tension or insecurity. Take a break and write down your successes no matter how small. Keep negative thoughts hidden away and focus on how well you've done.

7. Brainstorm alone or with a partner. When you brainstorm, write down anything that is remotely related. Be willing to be silly, and just list specifics. When you think of one word, it should lead to another word. This technique is effective for determining which angle you should cover when writing the article.

8. Try mapping. Mapping is a technique that allows many people to explore a subject more effectively with traditional outlines. Put the topic in the center of the page in a circle. Then as quickly as possible, draw lines out that follow the ideas that occur to you.

9. Keep a notebook or journal. Use it as a traveling office in which to scribble ideas, draft leads, brainstorm, map, record overheard conversations, list unexpected statistics, and carry on a continuous conversation with yourself about your work.

10. Compost. Keep a file drawer of reports, photos, speeches, brochures, handouts, newspaper clippings, letters, features, cartoons, ads, and magazine articles. Go through the file. You may unearth material that you've been collecting on topics that can make good stories.

9
Mechanics of writing

a. Grammar myths and misconceptions

In school, we were taught to avoid certain phrases and words, not because they were incorrect, but because we didn't use them correctly. Here are the realities behind some common notions about writing.

You *can* start a sentence with "because:"

> Because your company produces excellent newsletters, we want you to have our account.

Fragmented sentences were taboo. But sometimes, they can be very effective:

> They suggested we add a third color to our newsletter. Not a good idea.

It is acceptable to start a sentence with "and"

> This month's newsletter was late. That's the third time this year. And the phones were down again.

Some people object strongly to split infinitives. But they are not always inappropriate and can sometimes be better than the unsplit version. "To go boldly where no one has gone before" sounds odd.

> To boldly go where no one has gone before.

In most cases, sentences should not end with prepositions, but when Winston Churchill was accused of demeaning the English language, he replied:

> "This is a situation up with which I will not put."

It is all right to use "I" in an article, but sometimes a sentence is stronger without. "I think newsletters are a strong promotional tool" makes "I" the most important part of the sentence, but this is more direct:

> "Newsletters are a strong promotional tool."

b. Grammar and spell checker software

A grammar software program on your computer can improve accuracy by checking your articles for mistakes in grammar, style, usage, punctuation, as well as spelling. (See chapter 15 for more information on proofreading.)

One software program for computers is Grammatik which allows you to select one of six writing styles (business, technical, fiction, general, informal, or custom). Grammatik finds errors you might miss, including incomplete sentences, disagreement between subject and verb, improper usage, incorrect verb forms, incorrect pronouns or prepositions, inaccurate phrases, clichés, and jargon. It also spots mechanical errors such as doubled words, incorrect capitalization, punctuation, spelling, and number style.

Grammatik works with most word processors including MacWrite, Microsoft Word, WordPerfect, and Write Now. The easiest way to improve your writing retails for about $79.

Don't rely on computer spell checkers to uncover all errors in your articles. Most spell checkers are designed to spot misspelled words, but not incorrect words. A classic error I almost missed should have read "helpful tips to run your business," but instead I typed "helpful tips to ruin your business!" It passed the spell check because it was spelled correctly. It also passed a grammar check because it is correct.

c. A few grammar rules

1. Avoid verbs ending in "ize"

In recent years, the tendency to add *ize* to verbs has increased. Editors should use them with reluctance and only when no satisfactory alternative exists. Words such as accessorize, capsulize, decimalize, definitize, finalize, prioritize, and therapize are unnecessary.

The word hospitalize should be avoided as ambiguous, meaning both to send to hospital and to admit to hospital.

2. Avoid slang

Some writers have increased their use of phonetic spellings of common speech patterns including whassup, gonna, gotta, and wanna. Slang has its place. Dialects and slang are expected in fiction, plays, and movies but not in professional journalism. Good writing never calls attention to itself.

3. Omit meaningless words

At the end of a sentence containing a string of words or phrases separated by commas, many writers feel compelled to attach meaningless words to tell the reader, "This is an incomplete list."

The newsletter provides information about writing, content, style, design, typesetting, printing, and distribution, among others.

Tip: Delete the "and" before the final item.

The editor spends many hours writing, editing, managing, designing, producing, and similar activities.

Tip: Omit the last three words and add a period.

4. Open, solid, and hyphenated terms

A dictionary may provide the accepted spelling of compound nouns, whether open (field worker), solid (fieldworker), or hyphenated (field-worker). Hyphenate compound adjectives such as long-term investment, unless they are recognized as paired adjectives that usually modify the noun they are in front of, such as current account balance.

Run prefixes solid (i.e., without a hyphen), unless they produce unusual words like crosssectional or unless the prefix is attached to a compound word (non-oil-exporting) or a capitalized word (non-British).

Whichever spelling you choose, be consistent.

d. Punctuating properly

Many writers like to toss around dashes to keep things stirred up. Their appearance is more dashing than a crooked comma, the hangdog semicolon, and the obese parentheses. Dashes are frequently misused for other forms of punctuation.

The comma indicates a slight break in the sentence, the semicolon a rather large pause, and the dash an abrupt, dramatic turn. Dashes should be used sparingly; overuse weakens their effect. They often add a jarring note to an otherwise smooth sentence.

The dash is used correctly here:

> They walked along the path — dozens had tread before — until they reached their destiny.

This sample is incorrect:

> He told his teacher — who had a degree in journalism — it made no sense.

In the latter example, commas should be used instead of dashes.

Here's an example of using a dash as fake dramatics:

> The teacher said she left the room — without explanation.

This example should have used parentheses or commas instead of the dashes:

> The 1,200 subscriptions — priced at $85 a year — were mailed on the first day of the month.

Here's another example of dashes used instead of commas:

> The emergence of newsletters — over 400,000 in Canada — has provided additional income for many desktop publishers.

Avoid using the dash to save a sentence. If commas or parentheses are more practical, use them.

Sample #24 outlines punctuation marks and how they are supposed to be used.

Set punctuation the same as the word it follows. When a comma, colon, or period follows a word set in italic or boldface, the punctuation should also be in bold or italic, even if the majority of the text is set in roman.

Question mark
should be used with direct questions. Avoid using question marks in headlines which should be statements not questions. No space before.

Hyphen
joins two words together, or indicates where a word has been broken over two lines. Two hyphens are never used as in typewriting. No space before.

Exclamation mark
also called a screamer, it can be used at the end of exclamations. Avoid using it to add emphasis or in headlines. No space before.

Single quotes
are less intrusive than double quotes. Avoid using these for emphasis when italics will do. A space is added before a single quote, but none after.

Ampersand
is not a proper substitute for the word *and*. Don't use the ampersand in text matter, dialogue, or headings unless it is a proper name.

Comma
is used to separate items in a list or clauses in a sentence. If a clause is in the middle, the commas should come in pairs. No space before.

Dash
or en-dash is used in pairs – usually instead of brackets – to enclose a secondary thought. Note the space on each side. Used with dates: July 10 – 14.

Parentheses
are used to separate a clause attached to a particular word in a sentence. For parentheses within parentheses, use square brackets.

Quotation marks
are also called curly quotes or smart quotes. They are used to highlight direct quotations or add impact to pull quotes. Space before an opening quote, no space after.

Bullet
called a "blob" in England, is used to set off items in paragraphs. You should use a thin space or more between the bullet and the first word.

Ellipsis points
indicate an omission from quoted material. If in the middle of a sentence, leave a space on both sides. Treat ellipses like a word.

Long dash
often called an em-dash, is used instead of a dash—like this with no space on each side—but notice the big breaks in the text. No space before.

Semi-colon
separates two parts of a sentence which are distinct thoughts, but related. No space before, but add a space after. If the word before is bold, make this bold.

Inch marks
are used by amateurs instead of quotation marks. Avoid the foot mark for a single quote. Used for dimensions. 5'6". No space before, but add a space after.

COMMONLY MISUSED WORDS

Here's a list of words that are often misused; their correct meanings follow:

accept — receive or agree to

except — but

affect — to influence

effect — a result

alternatively — as an alternative

alternately — to go back and forth

continuously — without interruption

continually — repeated frequently

discard — to throw away

disregard — to pay no attention

disinterested — unbiased

uninterested — bored

economic — having to do with the study of economics

economical — money saving

healthy — state of one's health

healthful — good for your health

historic — important; take note

historical — concerning history

imply — to not say directly

infer — to figure out what someone has said

insure — to guarantee

ensure — a variation of insure, but not insurance

assure — to remove doubt

led — past tense of lead

lead — present tense of led

loose — not tight

lose — to misplace

Write and rewrite. After putting your thoughts on paper, read your article aloud. Quite often we use the wrong word.

10
Writing headlines

a. *Function of headlines*

Studies show that headlines are the second-strongest design element on a page. (A photograph or illustration is the most important factor for attracting attention.) Like an advertisement, a headline must pull a reader into the story.

The functions of the headline are —

- to attract attention to the article,

- to tell the reader "This is for you" or "This is not for you; read something else,"

- to describe the context of the story or column. Even regular columns need more than the usual standing head, like "Message from the President." They need a headline that says "Here's what this column is about," and

- to motivate and involve the reader. People need a reason or a benefit to read on. The headline is used to interest them in the text.

b. *Styles of headlines*

You can add variety to your publication by varying the styles of headlines.

1. Banner headline

The standard headline is generally written downstyle and typed flush left:

Newsletter students learn editing and design tips

2. Deck

A *deck* is a subhead or secondary headline below the main headline. It is usually smaller in type size and may be in italic or plain style.

Students study newsletter publishing
Course includes editing, design, production and printing

3. Kicker

Kickers use a short lead-in phrase to catch your eye. They're usually underlined or italic, half the size of the main head, and in a contrasting font or weight.

Students learn editing and design tips

Newsletter Publishing

4. Hammer

Hammer heads are the opposite of kickers. They start with a large, bold phrase to catch your attention, then add a wordy deck below. They're effective and appealing, but are usually reserved for special stories or features.

Newsletter Publishing
Students learn editing and design techniques

5. Slammer

A slammer is a two-part head that uses a bold face word or phrase to lead into a contrasting main headline. Most newsletters limit it to special features or jump heads.

Newsletter Publishing: Editing and designing

6. Tripod

A tripod has three parts: a bold word or phrase (often all caps) and two smaller lines of deck squaring off alongside. Like most gimmicky heads, it is usually used for features rather than hard news.

NEWSLETTERS: Course includes editing, design, production, and printing

7. Raw wrap

While most headlines cover all the text below (three-column stories have a headline across three columns), a raw wrap allows the text to wrap beside it. Use this style of head with caution, since you do not want to confuse readers. It's also known as a Dutch wrap.

Students learn newsletter publishing techniques

Students learn newsletter publishing techniques in a course which includes editing, design and production procedures. Typography, page layout programs, and word processing programs are included. Lunch is included with Saturday course. Fees are payable in advance, or at the time of registration. Registration will be between 7 a.m. and 9 a.m. Saturday.

8. Sidesaddle head

Sidesaddle heads are parked beside the story, rather than above. This is a good technique for squeezing a story into a shallow horizontal space. It can be typeset flush left, flush right, or centered.

Students learn newsletter publishing tips & techniques

12 terrific techniques for typesetting

Question: When typesetting a two-line headline in a newsletter, which line should be longer?

Answer: Ideally, the top line should be the longer one, because the two lines of text in the headline will direct the reader down into the body text. Of course, the sentence must break at a logical spot.

c. Writing effective headlines

Headlines are very important in attracting attention. They affect the overall tone of a story. Remembering significant details makes for better headlines. For instance, the point size or style of your headline tells readers which stories are most important, so choose wisely. Use active voice. Put the subject first, then the verb. Use short words and write in present tense to add punch. ("Basketball team wins game.")

Try to capture the essence of the whole story in one line. But if you have to have more that one line, write line for line; know how phrases will divide. For example "Ski team to / hit the slopes" reads wrong. Try "Ski team ready / to hit the slopes."

And be impartial. Avoid dramatics such as "Manager challenges hiring policies," if "Manager suggests new hiring policies" is true. As well, don't be cute. Puns or rhymes don't belong in serious journalism.

d. Tips for better headlines

Here are several methods of using headlines to describe the content, while qualifying the audience, and establishing motivated readership.

1. Promise readers a benefit

Promise your readers a benefit. Provide a remedy or solution to a problem. Your readers will get help, advice, hints, tips, solutions. You can expand on this idea by adding buzzwords like quick, easy, simple, foolproof, tested, proven, or guaranteed.

You can also promise your readers a reward. They'll be or become smarter/richer/sexier by reading this article. For example: "Discover how to earn $100,000 a year as a desktop publisher."

Don't worry about length. People will read up to three lines of display type (14 points and up), so if a headline requires 18 or 30 words to get the benefit across, it's okay.

2. News or announcement angle

Develop a news or announcement angle into the headline. Even "News about Desktop Publishing" is more intriguing than "Desktop Publishing." By using words like new, news, announcing, introducing, launch, and breakthrough, you will arouse curiosity to find out what's new.

3. Numbers

Attach a number to build readership and involvement. There's something about a number that no one can resist. That's why newspapers don't say "Many people killed in highway accident," but rather "42 people killed in highway accident." A number sounds more credible.

Promise your readers 12 Terrific Tips, Nine Helpful Hints, Eight Reasons Why, Four Headline Hooks, or 22 Devilish Devices. Avoid numbering the points within the text. That technique establishes priorities for your readers, and they may resent it. Use points instead.

4. Using questions

The use of questions as headlines is a cheap trick developed in primary school. If you ask the reader a question, he or she may respond with a big "No!!" The advertising industry has a saying: Don't ask a question in a headline. Period. Instead of "Interested in desktop publishing?" write "It's time you learned desktop publishing."

5. Secondary headlines

It is possible to have more than one headline. Secondary headlines or readership promoters such as kickers, quote-outs, and read-outs can also be incorporated.

COMMON HEADLINE LAYOUT ERRORS

Avoid the following 15 common typesetting and layout errors that significantly decrease the readability of headlines:

1. Typeface too light
   Heavy winds rage
   in southeast Italy

2. Insufficient leading
   Heavy winds rage
   in southeast Italy

3. Letterspacing and wordspacing too tight
   Heavy winds rage
   in southeast Italy

4. Letterspacing and wordspacing too loose
   Heavy winds rage
   in southeast Italy

5. Avoid all cap headlines

HEAVY WINDS RAGE
IN SOUTHEAST ITALY

6. Avoid outline typefaces

Heavy winds rage
in southeast Italy

7. Avoid shadow typefaces

**Heavy winds rage
in southeast Italy**

8. Avoid script, cursive or decorative typefaces.

*Heavy winds rage
in southeast Italy*

9. Avoid headlines of more than three stacked lines.

Heavy winds
rage in
southeast
Italy

10. Avoid reversing headlines out of a screened background, unless it is more than a 60% black screen.

11. Avoid surprinting headlines over a screened background darker than 30% black.

12. Avoid surprinting a headline over a photograph, especially dark portions of the photograph.

13. Avoid reversing a headline out of a photograph, especially across a busy background.

14. Avoid crowding a headline with text directly above and below.

15. Avoid setting a headline too close to the text above it.

11
Photographs

Photographs are the most important visual you can have in your newsletter. A good story-telling photograph can express more than a page full of text. Photographs add interest to your pages, set the tone of your publication, help establish priorities, reinforce important ideas, and distinguish one issue from another.

Studies show that when readers view a page, they usually look at photographs first, headlines second, and cutlines (also known as captions) third. If any of these three items seem interesting, readers will read the associated article.

Use quality photography and art. Think about your newsletter graphically before the layout stage.

a. Elements of good photography

A photograph that can "tell it like it is" has more impact on the reader than a thousand words. In effective photographs, the direction of the shot should face into the article, rather than look away from it. A news photographer has the ability to freeze action on the printed page. The best sports pictures are action packed; beads of sweat add that something extra like icing on a cake.

The subject of your photograph is very important. If you don't have an outstanding idea, not even the best photographer can save you. The best photographs arouse curiosity. Before-and-after photographs seem to fascinate readers. When possible show the end-result of your story or photograph.

Although four-color photographs cost about 50% more than black-and-white, they are 100% more effective. A real value.

b. Photo sizing

The size of a photograph communicates with the reader; important photos are usually larger than supporting ones.

Always add a caption to a photograph to give relevance to the image.

Treat photographs and borders consistently. If you cut the photo to the rule, treat all photos similarly. If you trim halftones (screened photographs) inside the border and leave a little white space between the photo and the border, be consistent with other photographs.

It is important to have pictures of people, but if you have rows of portraits (mug shots), they should be sized uniformly.

c. *Cropping photos*

Cropping lets you re-frame the image, creating a new shape that focuses attention on what's important and deletes what's not.

A photo or illustration can be cropped to fit into almost any space, regardless of the shape. See Sample #25 on cropping photographs.

As a rule, you should edit and crop photos first, before you dummy the story. Once you've made the strongest possible crop, then select a layout that suits the photo.

A good crop adds impact by making the central image as large and powerful as possible. It eliminates unnecessary air, people, or distractions from the background. A good crop leaves air where it is needed.

A bad crop amputates body parts (especially at joints: wrists, ankles, fingers) or cuts off appendages (golf clubs, musical instruments). A bad crop forces the image into an awkward shape just to fit a predetermined hole. A bad crop changes the meaning of a photo by removing important information. A bad crop violates works of art. Any artwork not printed in full should be labeled "detail." A bad crop damages the original photograph.

d. *Photographic terms*

1. Cutlines

We've all heard the cliché that a picture tells a thousand words. Most photos require some words to further describe the subject or action depicted.

Every photograph, chart, illustration, or graph should have a cutline. The cutline identifies the action, people, or purpose of the art, and persuades readers to take a second look. Readers generally look at the art, read the cutline, and look at the art again.

Cutline writing is similar to news writing. Both styles answer the questions who, what, where, when, why, and how. Concise writing in the present tense is more important in cutlines.

Cutlines are usually typeset with the same typeface as the body copy, but in bold or italics to visually separate them from the text. In addition, cutlines are usually set justified with the photograph or art. Sometimes, a thin rule is added beneath the caption to divide it from the body text.

Cutlines may be placed beneath, above, or beside the artwork.

2. Framing

There are dozens of fancy border tapes and frames available for desktop publishers and clip-art books full of decorative frames. Avoid the temptation to destroy an elegant photograph with a gaudy, glitzy border. Art and photos should be framed with thin, simple rules. Anything thick,

SAMPLE #25
CROPPING PHOTOGRAPHS

Before designing a page, decide how you will crop the photographs. Photos are cropped for two reasons. First, crop a photo to eliminate distractions and add focus to the most important portion of the photo. Second, crop a photo to fit the layout.

◄◄ This is an uncropped photograph. This photo could be cropped on the sides so that the focus is on the action.

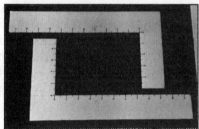

◄◄ Cropping Ls can be purchased from a photo supply store or made from a piece of cardboard. Use a marker to indicate inches.

◄◄ Lay the cropping Ls over the photo and decide where to crop. The inch marks help measure the finished size so you know how much the photo will be reduced or enlarged.

◄◄ The finished photograph is cropped tightly with unimportant "extras" removed. The focus of this photo is on the people and the photo album.

colorful, or decorative distracts the reader's attention from what's important — the photo.

3. Flopping

Printing a photograph backward as a mirror image of itself is called
flopping. When a designer wants a photo facing the opposite direction to
better suit a layout, the photo can be flopped. Flopping can be tricky to
use as it distorts the truth of the image. Avoid flopping news photos and
flop other photos only as a last resort. Make sure there's no way of telling
that you flopped it — watch out for clocks, writing, and other tell-tale
signs that will appear reversed.

4. Reshaping

Photographs work best as rectangles with right-angle corners. Cutting
them into other creative shapes distorts their meaning, confuses the
reader and messes up the page.

5. Tilting

If the artwork or layout justifies it, you may want to tilt a photo. When
thoughtfully designed, this is okay. However, beware: unless you choose
the appropriate art, tilt it at just the right angle, and skew the type
smoothly, you will trash the page.

6. Silhouetting

If a photo has harsh shadows or a distracting background, you may
consider cutting out the central image and running it either against the
white paper or with a new background. The technique works well with
some photos, poorly with others, but should be considered only for
feature pages.

7. Duotones

A duotone is a two-color halftone made from a regular black-and-white
photograph. Duotones are produced for two reasons. First, the full tonal
range of a good photograph is impossible to reproduce with a single
halftone. Using two negatives, printers can make one for highlights and
the other for shadows.

The second reason to use duotones is to achieve a special color effect
by combining two colors of ink. A dull photo can be made more dramatic.

Duotones are more expensive than simple two-color printing because
they require precise registration, and excellent stripping and press work.

8. Electronic photo manipulation

There's no doubt that electronic imaging (also called digital imaging, the
process of scanning artwork into a computer), has a serious effect on the
photographic process. As computer equipment becomes more powerful,
more accessible, and less expensive, much of what was traditionally done
by a photographer or airbrush artist, can now be handled on a computer.

Although unlikely to replace traditional photo processing methods, computers have become an increasingly important tool in photo labs.

The digital imaging process is simple. Images are first scanned into a computer. Once the images are in the computer, a photographic software program can be used to alter the photo. Adobe Photoshop, ImageStudio by Letraset, Aldus Digital Darkroom, and Micrografx Picture Publisher are the most popular image-editing software programs currently available.

For example, if a model had blood shot eyes, the desired shade of white can be electronically picked up from another part of the eye and used to eliminate the redness. Other applications can be performed including darkening, lightening, overlapping two photographs, removing flaws or seams, changing colors, altering locations, or eliminating distracting backgrounds.

To maintain the highest resolution possible, these images require an enormous amount of disk storage space.

Once manipulation has been completed, the image is generally output on a high-end imagesetter or linotronic equipment.

Your publication can cover a variety of topics with stories, artwork, charts, diagrams, maps, and photographs. Rather than describe the construction of your new office building, tell the story with a photographic spread. Here are a few suggestions for reporting stories and events with photographs.

PHOTOGRAPHIC IDEAS

- A day in the life of an employee or member
- A picture essay of organization activities
- A picture essay on how things are made at your company
- A photograph explaining service procedures
- Compare photos from ten years ago with current
- New employees or members
- Photo of winner doing the activity that made him or her a winner
- Promotions
- The organization's baseball or bowling team
- Display members' artistic projects or photographs
- People at the Top — Feature members, their job descriptions, interests, family life, etc.
- Photos of ex-members and what they're doing now
- A classroom photo of students or a boardroom meeting
- Before and after photographs attract much attention (The old building versus the renovation.)
- Tell a photographic story of how work is performed at your organization (Have a flow chart describe the activity with people doing it.)
- If your organization has a new logo, marketing plan or advertising campaign, perhaps you could show a collage of the doodles and notes leading to the finished concept.
- A day in the life of a woman performing a traditionally male activity or job — or vice versa
- "Who's who" — Feature photos of members as children and now. Readers can guess who's who.

12
Legal considerations

In 1990 David Swit, president of Washington Business Information, Inc. received a six-figure out-of-court settlement from a Fortune 500 company accused of illegally photocopying one of his newsletters. He received national attention for the suit.

Recently, Swit launched a suit against Collier, Shannon & Scott, a Washington law firm for "regularly and repeatedly" making multiple illegal photocopies of his newsletter Product Safety Letter.

Now Swit is suing Connaught Laboratories, a leading vaccine maker, for copyright infringement involving statutory damages that could amount to $1.5 million.

Newsletters are big business. You may think your employee bulletin is just a small publication, but there are many legal and financial aspects to consider. Should you copyright your newsletter or register a trade mark? Who owns the original artwork? How do you obtain permission to use someone else's copyrighted work? Can you trade mark your logo?

a. Copyright

1. What is a copyright?

Copyright, the right to copy, means that the owner is the only person who may copy the work or permit someone else to do so. It includes the sole right to publish, produce, reproduce, and perform a work in public.

The copyright notice shows the first year of publication and the name of the sponsoring organization or publisher follow the word "Copyright." You can use either the symbol © or spell out "copyright." The notice of copyright should go in the masthead. For example, the copyright notice for this book looks like this:

Copyright © 1994 by International Self-Counsel Press Ltd.

2. Who owns the copyright?

The author owns the copyright to the work unless he or she was hired or employed by some other person to create the work, in which case the employer is the owner, or if the author assigns the copyright to someone else.

3. How do you obtain copyright?

In the United States and Canada, copyright in an original work is automatically acquired upon creation, with certain provisions for citizenship.

4. Should you register your copyright?

If you anticipate legal proceedings, it is a good idea to register your copyright with the appropriate government office. In the United States, you can apply to the Copyright Office in Washington, D.C. In Canada, apply to Consumer and Corporate Affairs, Copyright and Industrial Design Branch, 5th Floor, 50 Victoria Street, Place du Portage, Tower 1, Hull, Quebec K1A 0C9.

b. Trade marks

1. What is a trade mark?

A trade mark is a word, symbol, or design, or a combination of these, used to distinguish the goods or services of a person or organization from the goods or services of others in the marketplace.

2. How do you differentiate trade marks from copyrights, industrial designs and patents?

Copyright deals with original literary, musical, dramatic, and artistic works. Industrial designs deal with original ornamentation of any article of manufacture. This includes any shape, feature, or ornamentation, the object of which is to produce an aesthetic effect. Patents deal with inventions including new and useful processes, machines, manufactures, compositions of matter, or any new and useful improvements thereof.

A trade mark registration is only effective for a certain number of years from the date of registration and is only valid in the country where it is registered.

3. What is a trade name? How is it different from a trade mark?

A trade name is the name under which any business is carried on, whether it be the name of a corporation, a partnership, or an individual. A trade mark identifies goods and/or services. The trade name identifies a business.

Companies, individuals, partnerships, trade unions, or lawful associations may obtain registration. In the United States, contact the federal Trade-Marks Office in Washington, D.C.; in Canada, contact the Registrar of Trade Marks in Ottawa. See also *Register Your Trade-Mark in Canada*, another title in the Self-Counsel Series.

c. Who owns artwork?

Prior to starting an assignment, be sure you have an understanding of the client's ideas, what style of writing or illustration is desired, the purpose of the art, and how and where it will be reproduced.

A written contract ensures that both parties understand the terms of the agreement. Before signing an agreement, be sure you know who owns the final artwork: the client or the artist. Some artists sell first rights to their work and maintain ownership, even though a client has paid for it. Many artists are excited and eager to get an assignment, but fail to discuss the legal aspects.

After the artwork has been printed, maintain a good filing system of all artwork, photos, type proofs, and negative film. You may be asked to print more in the future, or if the client refuses to pay his or her account, the art could be used as evidence, should a lawsuit occur.

According to the Code of Ethics and Professional Conduct established by the Society of Graphic Designers of Canada, a designer shall retain property rights to original artwork unless it is specifically purchased apart from reproduction rights.

By law, the artist or author of the work owns the copyright in it unless hired or employed by some other person to create the work, in which case the employer is the owner.

The use of written contracts is strongly encouraged by the Graphic Artists Guild. In their Pricing and Ethical Guidelines, a proposal should discuss the usage, ownership of rights, artwork, and credit lines. A sample contract would state:

> "The artist retains ownership of all original artwork, whether preliminary or final, and the Buyer shall return such artwork within thirty (30) days of use."

However, *Creative Business*, a newsletter produced in Boston, disagrees. The editors published a booklet, *Pricing and Billing Standards*, that concludes that most graphic designers and copywriters are paid for the work and the client owns the work. Period. But, for many illustrators and writers who are selling one-time rights priced according to exposure and royalty fee arrangements, it is still common for the artist to retain copyright of the work.

Consider who owns the artwork before you publish.

There are standard trade customs in the printing industry. If an artist supplies camera-ready artwork to a printer, it will be returned. Some printers may retain the art until the account has been paid in full. The negatives and plates used for the job are considered to belong to the printing company, unless you have an agreement to the contrary. They are usually stored up to three years, depending on the printer. If a paper plate was used, it would be discarded upon completion of the printed work. Your printed piece cannot be reproduced without your consent.

If you decide you want the negative film, negotiate this in advance and be prepared to pay for it. It's best to discuss it at the time of the original quote. Often, a printer may have the silver content removed from the film upon completion of a job. Your purchase order should specify stock, ink colors, quantity, bindery instructions, and special requests such as the return of artwork.

d. Permission to reproduce photographs

You do not need permission to photograph a person. You are generally free to take anyone's picture, whether that person agrees or not. However, a photographer may need a release to *use* someone's picture. A person's picture may not be used for purposes of trade or advertising without permission usually granted in the form of a model release (see Sample #26).

If you think you may use the photograph for commercial purposes, you will need the model's permission. Usually photographers have pre-printed model release forms that grant the right to use the photo.

A release frees the photographer from liability as long as the photo is used in accordance with the conditions. The release may contain information about types of use, the persons who are permitted to use the photos, and any payment that is made in return for the release being given.

Unless a release specifies that it is irrevocable, it can be revoked at any time by the person giving it, even though the photographer may have spent much time and money preparing the photograph.

Remember, it is not your intention at the time you take the picture that determines whether a release is necessary; it is the purpose of the photograph that is important.

Most people love to see their photograph in the paper. Whether they like it or not, you still have a legal right to snap photos, and in most cases to print them. But, there are exceptions:

- Courts, local laws, or private owners can ban your camera or recording equipment from courtrooms, museums, factories, or other private property. If in doubt, obtain permission first. Many churches prohibit picture taking during wedding ceremonies.

- Military installations and other public buildings may prohibit photographs. Photographing money is limited so that you don't try to reproduce the real thing.

- Avoid publishing photos of a private person or situation if it might offend a reasonable person.

- If the photograph may be used in advertising campaigns or other commercial purposes, ask everyone involved to sign a release. You do not need a release for a photo used for current news, educational, or informational purposes.

  Some photographers use a basic form that states the following:
  "For valuable consideration, I hereby irrevocably consent to and authorize the use and reproduction by you, or anyone authorized by you, of any and all photographs which you have this day taken of me, negative or positive, proofs of which are hereto attached, for any purpose whatsoever, without further compensation to me. All negatives and positives, together with the prints shall constitute your property, solely and completely."

- If you add a caption or touch up a photo, avoid possibilities of libel. If the caption damages someone's reputation, it had better be accurate and fair.

- Use common sense. If you print a photograph of a person at a rally who's supposed to be at work, it may be legal, but it's not wise. If in doubt, ask permission.

SAMPLE #26
MODEL RELEASE

AGREEMENT BETWEEN

_____
(name of photographer)
(hereinafter referred to as "the photographer")

- AND -

_____
(name of model)
hereinafter referred to as "the model")

The parties hereto agree as follows:

1. The model hereby consents to and authorize the use, by the photographer, and the photographer's respective representatives, licensees, successors and assigns, of any and all photographs that the photographer has taken of the model and of the model's property, and of any reproductions of them, for any purpose whatsoever, including, but not by way of limitation, the sale, publication, display, broadcast, and exhibition thereof, in promotion, advertising, trade, and art, whether apart from or in connection with, or illustrative of, any other matter, without any further compensation to the model.

2. The model agrees that the photographs, reproductions, and negatives thereof shall constitute the photographer's sole property, and that the photographer has the full right to dispose of any or all of them in any manner whatsoever.

3. As the photographer proposes to act on this consent forthwith, the model hereby declares it to be irrevocable; and the model hereby releases and discharges the photographer and his respective representatives, licensees, successors and assigns, from all manner of actions, causes of action, debts, accounts, contracts, claims and demands whatsoever which the model or the model's heirs, executors, administrators or assigns can, shall, or may have at any time as a result of any act, matter or thing whatsoever arising out of or in connection with the consent and authorization given by the model in this agreement.

IN WITNESS WHEREOF the parties hereto have executed this agreement.

If model is an adult:

_____   _____
(Signature of photographer)   **(Signature of model)**

Address and phone number of model   **If model is a child**
or parent/guardian_____   I represent that I am the parent/guardian
                                         of the above-named model. I hereby consent
_____   to the foregoing on the model's behalf.

_____   _____
                                         (Signature of parent/guardian)

_____
(Date)

- Reprinting photographs, cartoons, illustrations, or articles from other papers and magazines without permission is forbidden by law. Always seek permission first. A cute photo may be appropriate material in your newsletter, but you must get permission before you can reproduce it.

For more information about the legal aspects of reproducing photographs, see *Photography and the Law*, another title in the Self-Counsel Series.

e. Previously published material and quotations

Quotations are indispensable and lend authenticity. In his book, *The Craft of Interviewing*, Tom Brady explains quotes as "those brief, brilliant bursts of life." Unfortunately, many quotes are not brief and brilliant, but lifeless and verbose.

The best quotes are usually obtained on the run: a hasty comment from a harassed lawyer, a bureaucrat seeking cover from a barrage of words.

Direct quotations must reproduce exactly, not only the wording, but the spelling, capitalization, and internal punctuation of the original.

There are a few exceptions to make the passage fit into the syntax and typography of the work in which it is quoted.

- The initial letter may be changed to a capital or a lowercase letter.

- The final punctuation mark may be changed, and punctuation marks may be omitted where ellipsis points are used.

- Omit original note reference marks in a short quotation from a scholarly work. (Authors may insert note references of their own within quotations.)

- Any obvious typographical error may be silently corrected when quoted from a modern book, magazine, or newspaper. However, the original spelling or error should be preserved in a passage from an older work or manuscript source.

In summary, like other facts, quotes are not subject to revision. Once words are enclosed by quotation marks, they must be what the source said. Trying to "improve" a quote by changing or rearranging words is a high crime and misdemeanor. You can, however, fix minor grammatical errors or omit pure padding or meaningless repetition.

CAN YOU QUOTE SOMEONE ELSE'S WORDS?

Photocopying or using copyrighted material in print is legal in some instances. Here's a guide for writers and publishers about what's fair and what's foul.

Almost all of us have quoted or closely paraphrased or photocopied what others have written. It is possible to make limited use of another author's work without asking permission, and still not violate a copyright law.

To determine whether you need permission to quote, ask the following three questions:

1. Are you taking an author's expression? Permission is necessary to use the particular sequence of words that authors put in recorded form to express their ideas or explain facts. Ideas and facts themselves cannot be copyrighted, and are freely available for all to use.

2. Is the author's expression protected by copyright? Much expression is public domain and therefore, does not have copyright protection.

3. Does your intended use of the protected expression go beyond the bounds of fair use? If you practice fair use when using an author's copyrighted work, you need not get permission. When the intended use goes beyond the bounds of fair use, obtain permission before publishing. To determine fair use, ask yourself: would you mind if someone took it from you? The key factor is making any use limited.

Fair use has some basic guidelines:

1. Don't compete with the source. You can't use another person's protected expression if it might impair the market for the author's work.

2. Crediting the author doesn't give you carte blanche. Fair use and giving credit are not the same.

The less you take, the more fair the use. Avoid quoting more than 100 words.

Almost all of us have quoted or closely paraphrased or photocopied what others have written. It is possible to make limited use of another author's work without asking permission, and still not violate a copyright law.

13
Desktop publishing and some basic elements of design

a. Desktop publishing

The electronic production process, commonly referred to as desktop publishing (DTP), has eliminated many of the steps used in producing printed material.

Today's designer has to be skilled in many areas of production. Besides designing the newsletter, a designer may markup, typeset, proofread, scan artwork, prepare color separations, and coordinate final output. The jobs of many skilled tradespeople have been combined into one "super designer" who is responsible for the many phases of production.

b. DTP saves time and money

Today, fewer materials, tools, and equipment are needed to produce final artwork. The evolution of computers in the graphic arts industry has changed the way we produce camera-ready artwork. Some of the benefits of desktop publishing are the following:

- DTP shortens several stages of the production process.

- You don't have to hire outside typesetters or film houses.

- One good designer can replace several key players.

- You don't have to re-key articles into the computer.

- Changes can be incorporated quickly and less expensively.

- Less supplies are needed for producing camera-ready artwork.

Technological advancements have decreased the time, materials, and expenses required to produce camera-ready artwork. Hopefully, it won't replace the quality.

c. Camera-ready copy from the computer

Traditional methods of producing a page of a two-color newsletter required approximately 20 minutes for typesetting, 20 minutes for paste-up, and another 20 minutes to do spot color separations. With today's computer layout programs, that same two-color page design can be completed in 30 minutes, with fewer materials. Typesetting, layout, and spot color separations can be performed simultaneously and output on a laser printer. Most layout programs allow you to make color separations so that all of the black elements can be output on one page, and anything to be printed with a spot color is output on another sheet. When you take these two sheets to a commercial print shop, tell them one page is for black ink, the other page for spot color.

Desktop publishing has reduced the amount of materials required to produce camera-ready artwork. The typical laser printer has 300 dots per inch (dpi), so halftone screens look coarse. You can take a diskette with your document to a service bureau or print shop with imagesetting capabilities, and they can output your document on an imagesetter with 1270 dpi. The higher resolution produces better quality type and halftones.

Traditionally, journalists wrote the articles and graphic artists produced camera-ready art. Today, many journalists, especially internal newsletter editors, are laying out the entire publication.

How have computers affected design? Today's designer is required to know more and produce more of the work. Originally, a typesetter did typesetting, paste-up artists did paste-up, and color separators provided color separations. With the evolution of computerized artwork, designers are doing almost all of the production including typesetting, layout, and color separations.

d. Desktop publishing equipment

Hardware refers to the computer; software is the programs that can be purchased and installed on the computer. Peripherals are accessories that can be purchased to operate with the computer such as a modem, scanner, or external storage devices. Sample #27 shows computer equipment and peripherals that can be used to produce publications efficiently.

1. Central processing unit (CPU)

The central processing unit (CPU) is the main part of the computer that contains the microprocessor chips that do the actual processing. At the time of writing, low-end Macintosh computers have a 68000 microprocessor, while the fastest have a 68040 chip. In the IBM (or compatible) world, the fastest computer currently is 486 DX/80 MHz. The larger the number, the faster the chip processes information.

A CPU's internal performance is referred to as its clock speed or clock rate. Speeds are measured by the frequency with which the CPU fetches new instructions and are measured in megahertz (MHz). The older Macintosh Plus computer used a clock speed of 8 MHz, while the Macintosh Quadra 950 has a 40 MHz chip.

2. Color monitor

If you are considering purchasing a color monitor, you can choose an eight-bit color card to get 256 color combinations, or a 24-bit color card to get over 16 million combinations! If you produce or manipulate many color photos, a 24-bit color card will produce photo-realistic color. Obviously, a 24-bit color card costs more.

Bits	Colors	Comment
1	2	Basic monochrome display (e.g., Macintosh 9-inch screen)
2	4	Not often used, but possible on all color and grayscale Macintosh monitors
4	16	Fine for spot color; uses very little video RAM
8	256	Most common Macintosh II color mode; with color turned off, it produces photo-realistic black and white images
16	65,536	Often available as faster, less RAM-hungry choice for 24-bit color monitors
24	16,777,216	True color, viewable on the Apple High Resolution Color monitor and dozens of third-party monitors. Requires special plug-in video board on most Macintosh computers

In computer technology, a bit is the smallest piece of information that a computer handles. A bit is either on or off, one or zero, or black or white. They have two distinctively different states. The more bits you put together into a unit, the more combinations you can come up with. For example, two bits together offer four possible combinations: 00, 01, 10, and 11. If each combination of bits in a group represents a color value, then the more bits you bundle together, the greater the number of colors a bundle can represent.

DESKTOP PUBLISHING EQUIPMENT

A typical desktop publishing business that specializes in newsletter production would have a Macintosh or IBM computer and peripherals for a more efficient operation.

1. **Color desktop scanner** is used to digitize the color or black and white photographs, logos, illustrations, and artwork into the computer. This is a low-end 300 dots per inch (dpi) scanner that is suitable for reducing photographs, but may not have enough resolution to accurately enlarge photographs.

2. **Black and white scanner** with optical character recognition (OCR). This scanner digitizes logos, black and white photographs, and illustrations at 450 dpi. OCR is a software program that scans typewritten stories into the computer, eliminating the need for retyping. It can scan about 30 typewritten pages per hour, which is much faster than the average typist's typing speed.

3. **External hard drive** saves information on digital cartridges. If you plan to produce process color images for magazines, you will need more storage space.

4. **Fax modem or modem** transmits information from your computer through a telephone line to another computer or fax machine.

5. **Label printer** produces labels from a roll of self-adhesive labels.

6. **Light fixture with clamp** is fastened to the shelf and illuminates the copy stand.

7. **Central processing unit (CPU)** contains the computer's operating system. The one shown here is a Macintosh IIvx computer with 20 megabytes of RAM and an 80 megabyte hard drive.

8. **CD-ROM** is a built-in feature of this computer. A CD-ROM (Compact Disks — Read Only Memory) can optically read but cannot save information.

9. **Monitor** displays what is on the computer. This 16" high-resolution monitor also has a 24-bit color card. It is capable of producing 16,777,216 colors.

10. **Extended keyboard** has useful features such as function keys (F1) and Page Up/Page Down keys.

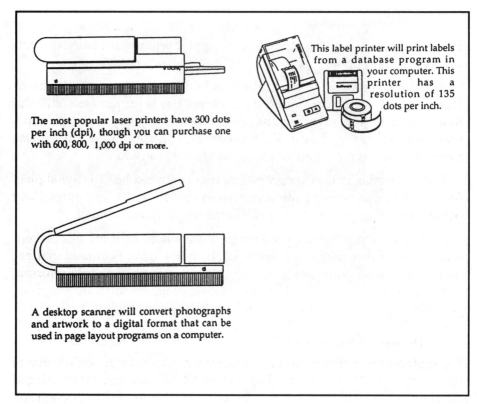

The most popular laser printers have 300 dots per inch (dpi), though you can purchase one with 600, 800, 1,000 dpi or more.

This label printer will print labels from a database program in your computer. This printer has a resolution of 135 dots per inch.

A desktop scanner will convert photographs and artwork to a digital format that can be used in page layout programs on a computer.

3. Laser printer

After reading a story or document on the screen, you will want to output it so you can proof it more carefully. There are basically four kinds of printers for personal computers: dot matrix printers, ink jet printers, laser printers, and color printers. Your decision will be based on price and quality of output.

4. Label printer

Some desktop publishers must generate self-adhesive pressure-sensitive labels for distributing a publication. Consider buying a label printer with a database program so you can create up-to-date labels. (See chapter 17 for more information on label printers.)

5. Modem

A modem transmits information from one computer to another through a telephone line. A fax modem will also send information from a computer to a fax machine. A modem is useful if your writer has a computer and wants to send an article "over the wire." You can also use a modem to transmit a finished page layout to a service bureau for final output. The cost of a modem starts at $200.

Sometimes, I don't even go to the service bureau. Instead, I send the newsletter file and all of the original scans by modem to the service bureau. This saves me time and reduces travel costs. When the imagesetting is done, I have a courier pick it up and deliver it directly to the printing house. Again, this saves me time.

6. Desktop scanner

Purchasing a desktop scanner for a computer will reduce halftone costs and production time.

You can scan logos, line art, black and white photos, color photos, or stories right into the computer. If the newsletter is output on a 1270 dpi imagesetter at the service bureau, the art is camera-ready and in position, ready for the printing house. With a scanner, you don't need a film house or print shop to create halftones and photostats for you.

Scanning allows you flexibility in incorporating images in your newsletter.

Images used in computer graphics programs must be in a digital pixel format. You can convert photographs to this format using specialized devices called scanners, digital still cameras, or video capture.

A scanner is similar to a photocopier; it bounces light off a document and converts the image to a series of very fine dots. Scanners that are intended for use with personal computers put these dots into a format that can be saved as a graphics file. With a graphics software program, you can import the file and edit the dots or copy the image.

(a) Choosing a scanner

The most common style of desktop scanner is the flatbed scanner, which was first introduced to the printing industry in 1982. When you lift the hinged lid, you see a glass plate, just like a photocopier. The artwork or photograph to be scanned is placed face down on the glass. The scanner usually comes with scanning software for your computer to scan the page. The scanning resolution (how many dots per inch you want the file to be saved as) is adjustable. The contrast between light and dark areas, and other settings can also be altered.

Color scanners work in RGB (red, green, and blue) colors only. Conversion to CMYK (cyan, magenta, yellow, and black) must be performed on a computer using programs designed for RGB to CMYK translations. Adobe Photoshop is an excellent software program for enhancing or transforming color photos. The program is available on both Macintosh and IBM (or compatible) computers.

(b) Optical character recognition

Some scanners allow you to use optical character recognition (OCR) software to scan pages of text into the computer. This will save you the time of retyping existing printed text into your computer.

To scan a document, lay it face down on the scanner glass, and then use the OCR software to scan the page. (I can scan about 30 pages of typewritten material in an hour. That's a lot faster than I can type!) After the text is scanned, it appears in a text editing window, which you can save to a disk file as a word processing document.

Accuracy of OCR software depends largely on the quality of the software and the clarity of the document it is scanning. Since OCR software tries to distinguish individual characters, blurry newsprint, very small print, or very light print may be difficult to decipher. (I discovered that nine point text or larger on white paper scans best. Fax transmissions don't scan very well.)

After scanning all your text pages, you need to use a word processing program to check spelling. Sometimes, "S" will be changed to "5," "O" to "0," and "I" to a "1."

Color flatbed scanners for computers start at $1,000. Hand-held scanners, which cannot scan full pages easily, are attractive for their comparatively low cost.

(c) Drum scanners

The drum scanner, or rotary drum scanner, uses a Plexiglas cylinder (drum) to hold copy being scanned. Since the 1970s, drum scanners have been producing the majority of all color separations produced in the printing industry.

Drum scanners are designed to separate photographs into red, green, and blue (RGB), or cyan, magenta, yellow, and black (CYMK) color. A drum scanner can produce an image in about 30 seconds per inch and can produce negative film much faster than a flatbed scanner. The flatbed scanner can take longer to produce negative film because three steps must be taken to get to film: the scan (three passes to get RGB), translation of the CMYK files from the RGB data using software, and the imaging of the film on an imagesetter. A flatbed scanner may be slower, but it is one-tenth the cost of a drum scanner. As well, now some flatbed scanners use only one pass to get RGB.

Training can be accomplished in a day because the machines are simple to operate, but color theory and press condition knowledge will take some time to understand.

(d) Choosing images for scanning

To get good scanning results, start with an image that's better in quality than one you will accept as the result. The best scans come from photographs and transparencies with good color, crisp focus, and clear detail. Sometimes the scanning process will lose information, so starting out with a photo that's already fuzzy will result in a very fuzzy scan.

The image should be free from scratches or other damage from faulty processing or mishandling. Dust should be carefully removed with a special brush or pressurized air available at photography stores. Damaged images should be replaced or retouched within an image-retouching program. A dust particle that is nearly invisible on a slide will be magnified when the image is enlarged and sharpened.

Study the image to see if it is too light or too dark. If so, you can make changes to the scanner's settings to partially correct the problem. By making a partial improvement on scanning, you have a better chance of capturing detail that may otherwise be lost.

(e) Tips for successful scanning

To obtain the best possible scan, there are several formulas you can use. When scanning a photograph, you need to know what line screen will be used in the printing process. Newspapers use a coarse screen of 65, 85, or 100 lines per inch (lpi). Magazines use a finer line screen of 100, 120, 133, or 150 lines per inch. For photos that will be used actual size, scan the photo with this dpi formula:

2 x lpi = dpi of scan

If you want a photo with 100 line screen, scan it at a resolution of 200 dpi.

When a black and white photo will be reduced or enlarged in the production process, use this formula:

$$1.5 \times lpi \frac{(WO \times LO)}{(WI \times LI)} = dpi$$

When a color photo will be reduced or enlarged in the production process, use this formula:

$$2 \times lpi \frac{(WO \times LO)}{(WI \times LI)} = dpi$$

W = width of photograph

L = length of photograph

O = output (final image)

I = input (original image)

For example, the original is a color 8" x 10" photograph. The end result will be 4" x 5" with 133 line screen.

$$2 \times 133 \frac{(4" \times 5")}{(8" \times 10")}$$

$$266 \times \frac{20}{80} = 266 \times \frac{1}{4} = 66.5$$

Scan the photo at 66.5 dpi.

(f) Saving scanned images

After you have scanned a photograph or artwork, you have to save it in a file format that can be "read" by your page layout program. For example, Microsoft Word, QuarkXPress, and Aldus PageMaker can import a variety of file formats including TIFF, EPS, or PICT. Remember: when you save a scan in one of these file formats, it cannot be opened; it must be imported into software that supports the format.

● EPS (Encapsulated PostScript)

The Encapsulated PostScript file format is used to export files to page layout programs. It was developed by Aldus to be used in object-oriented PostScript graphics. You can save an EPS or EPSF file as one composite file of RGB or CMYK images for output directly to color PostScript printers.

You can save a full 32-bit separated CMYK file as a five-file EPS file (see Chapter 5). This format saves the color separation information in a separate file for each of the four process colors. The fifth file is a low-resolution PICT image, known as a PICT preview, used to display the image in a page layout program. The four other files are linked to it; they always follow it wherever the PICT preview is saved.

EPS files are much larger than files in almost any other format. EPS files should be used primarily at the final stages of production to save storage space. The EPS format should be used mainly when you are dealing with full-color images. Because EPS files are very large, if you are working with grayscale images, you should place the TIFF format into page layout programs to save valuable storage space.

• TIFF (Tagged Image File Format)

TIFF or the Tagged Image File Format is the most common and one of the most flexible formats. Introduced by Aldus Corporation, it can be used on Macintosh and IBM compatible computers. Newer versions of TIFF support color and compression. The Tagged Image File Format also takes advantage of LZW compression. This compression, developed by Lempel, Ziv, and Welch (LZW), results in a smaller file size. But, not all page layout and composition programs can read these LZW compressed files.

• PICT

PICT is the internal format for storage and exchange of graphics documents on the Macintosh and the format used by the clipboard. Almost all paint programs read and write to the PICT format. This compatability enables you to exchange files freely between different Mac programs. The original PICT format was a one-bit-per-pixel format for MacPaint files. It now has 32 bits per pixel of color information.

• TARGA

The TARGA or TGA format is a standard for programs using the Truevision TARGA and Vista video boards. Primarily used in the IBM PC world, this format is useful if you plan to transport your images from Macintosh into PC systems. Many Macintosh programs enable you to save and read an image in the TGA file format. When you transport TGA files to other systems, you should remember that the file name must have a maximum of eight letters in the name plus a ".tga" suffix. When reading files from PC systems, be aware that there are several types of TARGA file formats, each of which has special considerations.

• RIFF (Raster Image File Format)

The Raster Image File Format is the default format of Fractal Design's ColorStudio program. The image file format works with 32 bits of information and includes options for compressing the file to save storage space. In most cases, you would not use the RIFF format in a page layout program. RIFF is useful in ColorStudio, but if you intend to use the image in other retouching programs, you need to save the image in one of the other formats.

- **Grayscale**

Grayscale is the representation of images using different levels of gray tone. Halftone images employ grayscale by varying the density of the halftone dots. Shades of gray on the screen are created by varying the intensity of the screen's pixels, rather than using a combination of black and white pixels to produce shading. Black and white televisions are grayscale. Most computer screens are not.

- **Photoshop**

This format is the default format used in Adobe Photoshop's image retouching program. Photoshop is a simple format that has no compression associated with the files. You can save the Photoshop format in a number of different color spaces from one to 32 bits. Photoshop is a clean, quick saving and loading format. But if storage space is a consideration, choose a different file format. In most cases, you cannot use this format in a page layout program. If you plan to use the image in other retouching programs, save the file in one of the other file formats. Photoshop can be read by the Scitex workstation, a prepress system.

- **Scitex CT (Continuous Tone)**

This image file format is used to export 32-bit CMYK or grayscale images into a format that the Scitex prepress workstation can read. This file format connects the Macintosh to a dedicated prepress system used by many professional color separators.

- **Crosfield CT (Continuous Tone)**

Like the Scitex CT, the Crosfield CT format enables you to export files that can be read directly by the Crosfield workstations.

Tip: When in doubt about the quality of your scans and separations, have proofs made to see what they really look like before proceeding to print.

e. Desktop publishing software

After purchasing the hardware for a desktop publishing operation, you must choose software programs that will work with you to produce satisfactory results. Five years ago, desktop publishers were advised to buy a word processing program, a page layout program, and a graphics program, because each program had a specific job. Today, programs are much more powerful, and sometimes one program will satisfy all your needs. Software programs are divided into nine categories, defined below.

1. Word processing programs

Type all documents with over two pages into a word processor such as Microsoft Word, WordPerfect, or MacWrite. Powerful word processors have a spell checker, grammar check, and thesaurus. Most layout programs can read these documents, so you can import a story into a page layout.

2. Page layout programs

QuarkXPress, Aldus PageMaker, and Ventura Publisher are the most popular layout programs for designing publications, advertisements, stationery, business forms, and promotional materials. You can import text from a variety of programs, graphics, or scanned images and arrange them on a page.

3. Graphics programs

Graphics or drawing programs are capable of transforming display type, creating logos, producing blends, and designing illustrations. The most popular graphics programs are CorelDRAW!, Adobe Illustrator, and Aldus FreeHand. Many clip art programs are created in Adobe Illustrator.

4. Photo imaging programs

In the past two years, the popularity of photo imaging software has skyrocketed as people alter photographs to achieve special effects or better reproduction. Adobe Photoshop, ImageStudio, and Digital Darkroom are common programs.

5. Database programs

A database program is good for maintaining lists or creating fill-in business forms. If you have to maintain a mailing list, a database program will let you sort it alphabetically by name, by region, by postal code, or by other information. FileMaker Pro and FoxPro are good database programs.

6. Spreadsheet programs

Spreadsheet programs like Lotus 1-2-3 and Microsoft Excel are excellent for recording numbers, producing tables, or creating graphs.

7. Integrated programs

An integrated program combines several programs into one. ClarisWorks and Microsoft Works have some word processing, some graphics, some database, some spreadsheet, and some communications abilities. Caution: These inexpensive programs are not usually as powerful as a designated program.

8. Accounting programs

AccPac Simply Accounting and Quicken are accounting programs that help you keep a set of books and produce financial statements for a company.

9. Miscellaneous programs and utilities

To maintain your computer or to have fun while computing, there are other programs such as Norton Utilities, SAM virus check, and After Dark.

f. Photo CD technology

Photo CD is a method of storing digital photographic images. Photo CD is an exciting new imaging techology developed by Kodak. CDs offer optical disk technology for commercial applications including computer imaging, image archiving and storage, image distribution, and image management. 35mm negative film and transparencies can be scanned to

CD. Some new computers come with a built-in CD-ROM, or you can buy a CD-ROM as a peripheral for your computer.

If you have a software program that allows you to import photographs, you can view your photographs on the computer. CD-ROM stands for Compact Disc-Read Only Memory.

When you take a roll of 35mm color film to your photofinisher, ask for a photo CD. Your film will be processed conventionally to produce negatives and a set of prints. Then, your film will be converted to a digital file, frame by frame, using a scanner. The scanned images are put into a high speed computer for color and density corrections, and then placed on the compact disc.

The applications for the photo CD are almost endless including catalogues, magazines, and educational uses. Photo CD technology is the storage system of the future.

g. Helpful hints for copyfitting

If you produce a newsletter regularly, you are probably familiar with the horrors of copyfitting. You either have too much text and not enough space, or too much space and not enough text.

A completed page layout can be wrecked by last minute editing. To avoid a total reset, try one or more of these options:

If the text is too long:

- Combine short paragraphs into one. This will decrease your overall length.

- Delete unimportant words from a paragraph. Avoid leaving one word alone on a line at the end of a paragraph.

- Use a smaller word to substitute for larger ones.

- Resize or crop graphics that take up too much space.

- Decrease space either between the lines or paragraphs.

- Rather than adding space between paragraphs, try indenting the first line of a paragraph.

- Reduce the point size of heads.

- Rewrite headlines so they fit on one line.

- Change the point size of your body text by a point or two.

- Instead of listing points in complete sentences, list key words with a bullet or number.

- Justify your text columns instead of using ragged right alignment. This may reduce several lines.

- Place the graphic at the beginning or end of the story, not in the middle.

- Decrease the size of your page margins slightly. This may eliminate a line or two.

If the text is too short:

- Add rules above and below your story.

- Increase the leading between lines and paragraphs to "open up" the page.

- Set your text ragged right instead of justified.

- Add subheads with extra space before and after.

- Use more graphics.

- Place photographs and artwork in boxes with drop shadows.

- Use white space effectively by deliberately using wider margins and columns.

- Use pull quotes (quote-outs) to take up space and lure the reader into the article. A pull quote in larger, bold type in a box will occupy more space.

- Reset the opening lead in larger type for a more dramatic opening.

- Enlarge artwork.

- Rewrite headlines to stack on two or three lines.

h. Using files from another computer

Writer Jim uses WordPerfect on an IBM computer to write his stories. Newsletter designer Kim used QuarkXPress on a Macintosh computer to lay out the pages. How do we get an article from one computer to a layout program on another computing platform? In addition, Jim's office is in downtown Toronto and Kim's is in San Francisco. What's the most efficient way of getting the article from Toronto to San Francisco?

Here are five ways to cross platforms or cross miles:

(a) Writer faxes hard copy of story to designer who retypes it into her own computer.

(b) Writer mails hard copy of story to designer who uses a scanner with optical character recognition to scan the story into the computer. The scanned story is opened up into a word processing program and spell checked.

(c) Writer ships diskette to designer and designer converts the language from WordPerfect (for IBM-based system) to Microsoft Word (for Macintosh) through a disk conversion program.

(d) Writer takes diskette to a service bureau for conversion. (Make sure you supply a blank diskette or they will charge extra.) The converted diskette is then mailed to designer.

(e) Writer saves story as ASCII text and sends it by modem to designer. For this method, both parties must be familiar with communications software and the technical problems associated with modems.

i. Elements of good design

The front page is the most important and should be given the most consideration. After all, that's the first page a reader sees. Try to have at least four items on the front page including a nameplate, inside box, and two stories. The nameplate identifies the publication and sets the tone. The "inside" or "contents" box promotes articles that appear inside and adds graphic relief to the page. I feel it is better to have two articles start on the first page and continue inside for two reasons: a continued story draws a reader inside, and black headlines help to visually break up a "gray" all-text page.

Readers observe the right page first, the left page second in a sideways U-pattern and often skip the middle, because of the fold. Design your pages with this in mind.

Standing heads or column heads identify regular columns, as well as provide graphics to the page design. Consistency in layout design, style, and page content is important. Strive to keep regular columns on the same page, so that readers can find their favorite columns easily.

It is up to you as the publisher to encourage the maintenance of standards of good design.

j. Color, design, and content affect readability

There's no doubt color and compelling design attract readers to news pages and advertising, but it's the editor's imaginative approach to articulating and presenting the news that makes the difference.

The editor also contributes to the design of a newsletter.

Readers don't automatically look at the top right-hand position for the "lead" story. They enter the page wherever the most eye-arresting element is. And they are willing to follow trails editors mark for them.

When looking at facing pages, readers first perceive them as a single unit, not as two separate pieces. Their attention tends to move from right to left. Readers view facing pages through a dominant photo on the right-hand page and move to prominent headline or another dominant photo.

Color screens over text seem to have little effect on readership.

Readers may tolerate a bolder use of color than editors and designers have assumed. Readers seem to prefer colorful pages over more muted tones. Color doesn't necessarily draw more attention, but readership increases as illustrations become larger.

Readers tend to be scanners, looking at only 25% of the text and reading in depth no more than half of that.

Sample #28 shows basic design elements that aid in readability.

k. Use visuals — PIGs

Every good newsletter needs at least one PIG per page. That is, try to have at least one photograph, illustration, or graphic on each page.

Infographics such as charts, graphs, diagrams, tables, and maps are important elements of newsletter design. Charts and diagrams demonstrate the information in the article, as well as add to the visual appearance of your page. An attractive page layout is essential to producing an effective, reader-friendly newsletter. Graphs and tables will also aid readers in understanding your statistics.

Like photographs, good visuals need cutlines to explain the action in the visual. Call-outs draw attention to the most important features of a diagram or chart. Call-outs are rules or arrows that point to something in the diagram, accompanied by a brief description of the part, benefits, or features. Call-outs help educate readers by providing a brief synopsis of the illustration.

Photographs are vital components in a successful newsletter. They help break up copy, attract attention, and illustrate the article. Although it is important to include people in your photos, avoid clichés such as the executive talking on the telephone and "grip and grin" photos. For more ideas for your photographs, refer to chapter 11.

Tip: If you can place a dollar bill on an area of text without covering any visuals, then you have too much text. Your body copy is calling for attention.

My Nameplate

Month, Year   (10 point Helvetica)   Tagline or descriptive copy   Issue Number

24-pt Helvetica bold headline

Major stories will have a 24-point Helvetica bold headline. Secondary stories will have 18-point headlines. Fillers and personal notes will be 14 point.

Headlines will be written with only the first letter capitalized. All other words, except proper nouns will be in lowercase letters.

Text will be 10-point Palatino with 12 points of leading. Drop caps at the start of a story are equivalent to three lines of type.

Paragraphs will be have one pica indents without extra leading between them.

Format will be 11" x 17" folded to 8.5" x 11".

The grid will be three columns. Columns will be 12.5 picas wide with 1.5 pica alleys.

12 point subheads

Subheads will be in 12-point Helvetica bold to add contrast from the body text. There is an extra six points of leading above and below the subhead.

All photographs, illustrations or charts will have a 0.5 point border to add a polished, professional appearance.

The by-line, or author's name, will be 10-point Palatino italic, flush right.

Stories will end with a 7-point, outline square with shadow. ▫

Author's By-line

Photo Credit: 8 pt. Helvetica

Captions will be 10-point Palatino bold with two points of leading (12/12). Placement will be below the photograph, chart or illustration and set justified.

Secondary stories will have 18-pt Helvetica bold headlines

Page numbers will be placed along the bottom of a page in 10-point Palatino. Even pages will have a page folio on the outside, left side, while odd pages will have a page number on the outside, right side.

Each page will have a 0.5 point border, which is four picas from all edges of the page.

Column rules between columns are 0.5 point.

Cut-off rules between stories are four point.

The inside box to the right will have a 0.5 pt. border and a 10% screen. The inside heading is 12-point Helvetica bold. The listings in the box will be 10-point Helvetica, double spaced. A dot leader is used to connect titles and the page folio. The folio is bold.

Text for all stories will be 10-point Palatino with 12 points of leading. Drop caps at the start of a story are equivalent to three lines of type. ▫

INSIDE

Inside heading
will be 12-point type
Helvetica bold...........................1

Listing in the box
will be 10-point Helvetica,
double spaced.........................2

A dot leader
is used to connect title
and page folio.........................3

DTP MISTAKES TO AVOID

- Using underlining or capitals for emphasis instead of bold or italic type
- Two spaces after a period
- More than two typefaces in a publication
- All capital letters in headlines
- Too much space between the letters in the headlines
- Outline and drop shadow type which is thin and difficult to reproduce
- Trapped white space as a result of poor layout
- More than two line thicknesses in a publication
- No grid or different grid on every page
- Rivers of white space
- More than 55 characters per line
- Columns more than 42 picas wide
- Type size too small (in order to fit more on a page)
- Inconsistent headline size
- Headlines for important stories are smaller than those for fillers
- Text inside a box without a margin between text and frame
- More than two initial caps per page
- Less than 50% of page is white space
- Body copy reversed
- The use of "ticks" instead of real "quotation marks"
- The use of two hyphens instead of an em-dash

14
Using traditional methods

a. *Copy preparation*

1. Mark-up

Copy preparation is also referred to as mark-up. The original copy is given to the typesetter with instructions on setting the typeface, type size, leading, justification, and other special requests. Sample #29 shows double-spaced copy that has been marked up for typesetting.

2. Layout

Often, a mock-up version of the layout is created to show what the finished artwork should look like. It is usually created to scale and marked-up for typesetting. If the newsletter will be typeset and pasted-up in the traditional manner, a mock-up shows the paste-up artist where the type and artwork should go. In desktop publishing, the copy may be typeset and the page laid out at the same time on the computer. In larger studios or with larger projects, one person may typeset the copy, save it as a text file, and pass it to the desktop publisher who positions the type on the page according to the supplied layout. Sample #30 shows a mocked-up layout with typesetting instructions.

Once the articles are written, photographs taken, and pages designed, it is time to produce camera-ready copy that can be printed. In the design and planning stages, you established a grid for your publication and decided how many columns for each page. How will your articles and artwork be laid out? Your commercial printer or typesetting house could do the typesetting and layout, or you could hire a graphic designer to produce the camera-ready copy for you.

Camera-ready copy or camera-ready art refers to typesetting and artwork that is ready for the process camera to make negative film. The film is stripped up and used to make printing plates. The plates are used on the printing press to produce your printed material.

b. *Typesetting*

Today, you can purchase a computer, laser printer, scanner, modem, typefaces, and software for under $10,000. Desktop publishing is an ideal business to operate out of your home because it's not messy. There are no chemicals, photosensitive papers, or massive pieces of equipment.

In the 1990s, most typesetting companies have bought computers and produce type and layouts at the same time. The whole graphic arts

This is a sample of an article that has been prepared for a typesetter or commercial printer. Notice how it is typed double-spaced with wide margins. It is easier for a typesetter to type when the lines are spaced out. It also gives an editor space to make changes. This copy has been marked-up with instructions on how it should be typeset. The headline should be 36 point type on 34 points of leading, using the typeface Helvetica and the style is bold. The headline will be typeset with upper and lowercase letters, flush left, ragged right. Three lines under a character symbolizes it should be an uppercase letter, while a slash through a capital letter indicates it should be typed lowercase. A line break is indicated between the words "good copy" and "preparation" so that "preparation" will appear on the next line of type. The body copy will be typeset [m24 which means flush left on a measure of 24 picas. The width of the body text shouldbe typeset 24 picas wide.

36/34
Helvetica bold
u & lc
[flush left
ragged right

GOOD COPY PREPARATION

When preparing copy for a typesetter or printer, it is important to supply clean copy. Copy should be typed on standard 8.5" x 11" bond paper, and on one side of the sheet only. Use a 6" column so that you have a generous margin. The type should be double-spaced. Every page

10/12
Helvetica
u & lc
[m24
flush left
ragged right

should contain the same number of lines. Make sure all pages are numbered consecutively to avoid confusion if the sheets get separated. Also, make sure the job title appears at the top of every page to prevent the copy from being mixed up with another job. Write your typesetting instructions clearly in the left-hand margin, using the standard set of proofreaders' marks. Learn these proofreading marks: they are brief, clear, and they convey your instructions efficiently. Most typesetters will follow only the instructions you give them; you cannot expect them to make design decisions. The responsibility for these decisions, and for clearly directing the typesetter, is yours and yours alone.

Provide a layout to the typesetter or commercial printer showing what you would like. This layout could also be called a comp of the copy to be set. It is marked-up to indicate what typeface and type size should be used.

36/34
Helvetica bold
u & lc
flush left
ragged right

Good Copy Preparation

10/12
Helvetica
u & lc
[m24
flush left
ragged right

14/16
Helvetica bold
u & lc
flush left
ragged right

Step One

industry has been affected by the evolution of desktop publishing. Organizations that used to hire outside companies to typeset and layout their newsletters are now doing the entire production in-house. Newsletter editors who wrote the articles and farmed out the production are now laying out an entire publication. A PostScript laser printer purchased for under $2,000 can output business forms and reports suitable for printing.

1. The photocomposition process

A typesetting machine is similar to a typewriter, with an operator "typing" the copy into the machine that automatically sets the type and justifies it. It is also like a camera with four basic parts:

(a) A lens

(b) An aperture through which a strong light exposes the sensitized paper

(c) An alphabet and other characters on a negative strip of film, so when light shines through the film, the type character forms on the sensitized paper

(d) A holder or cartridge for the photographic (sensitized) paper

A typographer selects the type for the newsletter, book, brochure, or advertisement. The machine remembers the characters line by line as they are typed on the keyboard. When the return key is pressed, the characters are photographed on paper. When typesetting has been completed, the paper is developed, usually by a photostabilization process.

Photosensitive paper is stored in a light-tight supply package inside the machine, but is exposed to receive the typeset image. It then goes into a light-tight cassette.

2. Keyboard

Some photocomposition units have a keyboard like a typewriter, but with additional characters and functions. When type is being set, the characters and functions will show on the control panel visual display.

3. Developing the images

When the typesetting has been completed, the paper feed key is pressed to clear the type from the machine and store it in the cassette. The cassette can be removed and placed in the photostabilization processor. This is a rapid process of developing photographic prints. The paper already has the developer in the emulsion. In seconds, two chemical baths will produce an image automatically. The processor has to be cleaned regularly and fresh chemicals added.

c. Dry transfer method

Dry transfer type can be purchased from art supply stores. By burnishing or rubbing, a letter can be transferred from the font sheet to a layout sheet. This is a slower process, as each character must be burnished individually. It is only used for display lines, headlines, and for single words. Type from font sheets can only be used once, but you can purchase sheets in most sizes and typefaces.

d. Paste-up

After the headlines and articles have been typeset, the galleys are pasted into position. The artwork may be waxed, glued, or taped onto artboards, paper, or acetate to create camera-ready art. Most paste-up artists use semi-permanent wax on the back of typeset galleys because it can be repositioned if necessary.

Many printers and designers have paste-up sheets custom printed for their newsletter. The newsletter grid and ruled guidelines are printed with non-repro blue ink on a lightweight, coated stock. Light blue ink is used because a process camera cannot see light blue when negative film is shot. Therefore, the guidelines will not reproduce.

Paste-up artists usually start at the top or the bottom of a page, by choosing a "squared" story first. A "squared" story has columns of equal length, so it is easier to paste up. If a story is shared between two columns, carefully fold the galley in half to determine the mid-point, and cut it apart. You can also use a printer's gauge to measure the length of the story to determine the mid-point. A story spread over three columns can be measured and divided into three equal pieces.

If a computer layout program isn't available to you, traditional paste-up methods can result in a professional-looking newsletter.

Headlines are usually placed right above the story and span the length of the columns. A three-column story will have a headline that goes across three columns. When positioning a headline above a story, the headline should be closer to the story it belongs to. Many artists incorrectly center a head between two stories. Strive to have more space above the head and less below. This will aid readers in realizing this headline belongs to this story. Sample #31 shows final paste-up for artwork.

e. Indicating color

There are three methods of indicating color and other instructions to a printer. First, you could photocopy the art and write printing instructions on it. Second, you could tape a sheet of tissue paper to the art and indicate instructions on it. And, third, you could separate the colors yourself.

Mechanical art is artwork prepared by a designer with overlays showing each color to be printed: one overlay for each color in exact register with the base artboard. The black text (or main color) may be on the base artboard, while each color is on an acetate overlay. For example, if you have a blue spot color, you would place all blue elements — rules, text, logos, and art — on an acetate overlay. Any element that is to be printed with red ink is placed on another overlay. Registration marks are added to the base art and to each overlay to register the colors.

If you want a tint block or screened box, you could indicate instructions such as "20% blue screen" to the process camera operator. You could also do your own mechanical art by taping a sheet of amberlith or rubylith to the artboard. Amberlith is basically clear acetate with a colored layer or film on top. If you want a screened box, you use a sharp knife to cut through the top layer of film. All of the colored film around the box would be removed, leaving the clear acetate with a solid, colored box. The

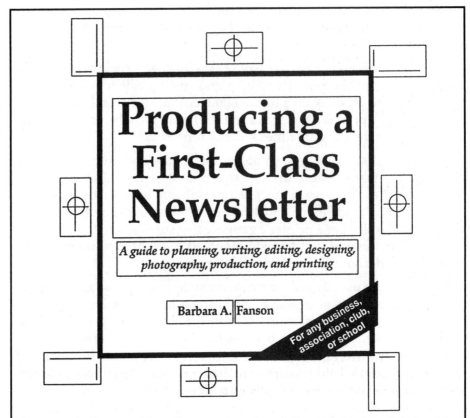

Paste-up is the assembly of items to be printed. Several steps are involved in creating this example:

1. Use a non-repro blue pencil to draw the dimensions: 4.5" x 4.5".

2. Add trim marks to each corner to indicate the outside edge. They can be applied with a black pen, border tape, or dry transfer lettering.

3. Registration marks are added if this will be printed with more than one color of ink.

4. Use six-point border tape to create the border on the inside of the guides.

5. Apply wax to the back of the typeset paper and place the waxed paper on a cutting mat.

6. With a knife and printer's gauge, cut the type.

7. Place each piece of type in position. If you draw a guideline to represent the horizontal center, your type will be easier to center. Carefully fold each slip of type to find the center of the type.

8. Use a process camera to reverse the type for the slash bar.

process camera operator, stripper, or printer will produce the screen from your overlay.

f. Sizing artwork

Sizing photographs, illustrations or logos is easy with a proportional scale. Buy one at any art supply store. Line up the inner wheel (original size) with the outer wheel (reproduction or desired size) to calculate the percentage of the reduction or enlargement. For example, if you have a photograph 6" wide and you want to reduce it to fit in your 2" wide column, line up 6 (original size) with 2 (desired size) and the proportional scale will show 33%. The printer or process camera operator will reduce the photo to 33% of the original size.

You can also use a calculator and this formula:

$$2 \times \frac{100\%}{6} = 33.33\%$$

g. Photo reproduction

To the designer, copy usually means typewritten copy that has been marked-up and typeset. To the printer or platemaker, copy means anything that is to be printed: type, photographs, illustrations, charts, rules, etc. All copy can be divided into two categories: line copy and continuous-tone copy.

1. Line copy

Line copy is any image that is made up of solid black, with no gradation of tone including rules, dots, solid masses, etc. The type you are reading is line copy. Line copy is shot with a high-contrast film by a process camera that reduces everything to either black or white. The film is developed, producing a line negative that can be used to make a plate.

2. Continuous-tone copy

Continuous-tone copy is any image that has a full range of tones from white to black. Photographs, paintings, charcoal drawings, and pencil drawings are all continuous-tone copy since they contain many gray tones between black and white. Because a printing press cannot put ink on lighter in certain areas, the photograph is screened into a series of dots. The screen placed over the film or paper during exposure has dots that are evenly spaced but vary in size. In light areas the dots are very small and in the dark areas, very large. The press can print these dots.

h. The process camera

After the typesetting and paste-up have been performed, the "camera-ready art" is ready for the process camera. This large camera will photograph the artwork to get a negative. Any type or art in black on the paste-up will become clear on the negative.

A *line negative* is a film of all images that prints solid lines and shapes on the paper. It can include ruled lines, spots, line drawings, and type.

A *screened or halftone negative* is used for a photograph. The screen breaks the image up into a dot pattern.

A *duotone* is a halftone printed in two colors. Two halftones are made from the same photograph except that the screen angle is changed for one.

Posterization is exposing continuous-tone copy as though it were line copy. A contact screen is not used during exposure. Usually the color negative is underexposed while the black negative is overexposed.

A *PMT* (photomechanical transfer) is an enlargement, reduction, or same size print of artwork or logo. It is done for artwork and saves the original art. PMT negative paper is exposed in the process camera and fed into a processor with a receiver, or positive sheet. In 30 seconds, they can be separated and an image appears on the receiver.

A PMT is a much higher quality reproduction than a photostat or photocopy, but at 10 times the cost. A PMT is a positive image produced with a process camera onto photosensitive material, whereas a photostat or photocopy uses a dry ink process onto paper. If image sharpness is your most important consideration, consider getting a PMT. If a high contrast, medium-sharp image is acceptable, then a photostat or photocopy will be sufficient.

If you photocopy a photograph, the result is a high-contrast print. Your print has blacks and whites, but no gray tones. Letraset manufactures a copy sheet that you can place on the photocopier with the photograph to produce better screened prints. Although the quality is not as good as a halftone PMT, the photocopied photo is acceptable.

i. Typesetting on photographs and screens

1. Surprint/overprint

A surprint is a solid color (type or line art) superimposed over a halftone or screen of the same color. It is produced by the double-burning method: exposing a second negative (type or art) upon a previously exposed first negative (halftone or screened background). The result is one negative used to make one plate, thereby printing the image in one ink color.

An overprint is a solid color printed over a different color halftone or screen. It is produced with two separate negatives and two separate printing plates and run with two different ink colors.

Remember: a surprint is solid color printed over the *same* color background; an overprint is solid color printed over a *different* color background.

2. Dropout/reverse

The terms dropout or reverse are easily confused because they have almost the same effect: light type or art against a dark background. A dropout refers to an absence of color within a screened color area. A dropout is produced by masking out areas of halftone dots with a film positive of black type or art. The film positive (black type or art) is placed over the halftone, and the two pieces of film are double-burned. The black areas do not permit dots to be formed there, so the result is a "clear" area without dots, the dropout area.

A simple reverse (white type of art against a black or other one-color background) is produced by making a negative of the original (black type or art on a white background.) A film positive is made of the negative film (now white type or art on a black background) and exposed to a printing plate. When printed, the result is white type or art on a black (or other one-color) background. The middle steps could be eliminated by preparing the original with white type or art against a black background. In desktop publishing, it is quite easy to make a black box and change the color of the type to white.

TEN TIPS FOR COPY PREPARATION

Before submitting your articles and photographs to a desktop publisher or printer for preparation into camera-ready artwork, double-check the following items:

- Nothing is missing.
- There is nothing extra.
- Instructions are accurate, specific, and easy to understand.
- Illustrations and photographs requiring halftones or stats have been sized and organized.
- All illustrations and photographs have been keyed to the right spot on the layout. (For example, write an "A" on the back of the photograph and then write an "A" on the layout so that your designer knows which way is up.)
- All artboards or pages are covered with a sheet of tissue, paper, cover sheet, or folder for protection.
- The name of the job, your name, and your phone number are on all pieces.
- Camera-ready artwork is accompanied by an instruction or production sheet.
- The dummy (layout) is included (if you have one).
- The delivery address is included.

15
Proofing

a. The importance of proofing

Proofing can save you a great deal of disappointment and embarrassment. Maintain high standards and earn a reputation for having a 100% correct newsletter.

Proofreading involves checking the detail, meaning, spelling, grammar, and style of an article. A well-designed newsletter loses integrity when a reader finds incorrect word usage or typographical errors. Too many errors and you'll turn readers off; they won't take your publication seriously.

b. Three proofing stages

A typical print job will be viewed in three different stages: as typesetting and artwork, as film, and as printing plates. At each stage you can inspect a variety of products called proofs.

During the production of a newsletter, there are several proofing stages to check the accuracy of your work. You can avoid feeling confused by knowing how to ask for the right proofs.

As a printing job progresses from concept to press, the proofs take longer to make. They represent the finished product more accurately. You also pay more to make changes. Many production managers use the 5-50-500 rule: It costs $5 to correct a mistake on a computer, $50 to correct the same mistake when discovered on a blueline, and $500 when it's found on an overlay or laminated proof. To correct an error found during a press check requires time and money.

1. From computer

(a) Viewing on screen

Many errors can be detected on your computer screen. Most computer programs contain a spell check feature and some also contain a grammar check. Most people prefer to proof from a printout. See chapter 9 for information on computer software that checks grammar errors.

(b) Black and white laser proof

A laser output of your document is very accurate for showing your type, screen tints, and photos in position. In many computer programs you can make color separations when you print. Each color will output onto a different sheet of paper. All black type and graphics will be printed on one sheet of paper and each spot color will be output on another sheet. Printing color separations on your laser printer will ensure that the right colors appear on the right separation. The cost: pennies.

(c) Desktop color proof

Color printers range from relatively inexpensive laser or thermal wax printers to costly dye-sublimation and ink jet devices. Accuracy usually increases with cost. Advertising agencies, prepress services,and printers usually have more expensive and accurate color printing machines. Cost: $5 to $35 per page.

(d) Imagesetter output

Imagesetting machines output pages with a higher resolution. The most common laser printers have 300 dots per inch (dpi). Imagesetters have 1270 dpi, 2540 dpi, or 3386 dpi. The more dots per inch, the better the resolution. Since most companies cannot afford to purchase this high-end equipment and hire trained operators, they can send their projects to a service bureau or commercial print shop for output. A service bureau will charge $6 to $20 per letter-sized page or $12 to $20 for a two-page spread. You can also have your artwork output directly to negative film. (Ask your print shop about film specs.)

Examine your output for obvious problems such as font substitution, incorrect screen angles and rulings, missing elements, and incorrect imposition. Check spot colors to make sure they're in register. If you have negative film made, check it by looking at the blueline proofs. Cost: $6 to $20 per page.

2. From film

If you are printing more than 1,000 copies, your print shop will probably need negative film to make metal plates. If you have less than 1,000 copies, the print shop may use paper plates that don't require negative film. There are several kinds of proofs made from film.

(a) Blueline

After the stripping process, you will want to check a blueline proof (sometimes referred to by the brand name, Dylux). If your photographs were stripped into the negative film rather than scanned into the computer, make sure that each photo is in the correct location and that each photo has been cropped satisfactorily. A blueline proof is usually folded and trimmed to represent the final product. You should also check creep, incorrect imposition, or wrong trims. Cost: $10 to $30 per page.

(b) White print

To check the tonal range of halftones (screened photographs), ask for a white print, often called by the brand name Velox. A Velox or contact print can be made from either loose or stripped film. Cost: $15 to $40 per page.

(c) Overlay proof

Overlay proofs consist of a set of transparent acetate layers, each with the image from one piece of film or one color. In a four-color process job, there is a sheet of cyan, magenta, yellow, and black. Overlay proofs are known by brand names such as Color Key, Cromacheck, and Color Check. Cost: $25 to $50 per page.

(d) Laminate proof

A laminate proof is the most accurate film-based proof of color. Known by brand names such as Matchprint, Cromalin, Agfaproof, Color Art, and Signature, they consist of transparent layers laminated to backing material. Each layer represents the film for one color. The result is a crisp, bright, laminated simulation of the printed product. Color separators, printers, and some service bureaus can make laminate proofs. Cost: $40 to $75 per page.

3. From printing plate

Sheets inspected at a press check are press proofs. Press proofs, also called press sheets, show how the job will print using the same paper, ink, and press as the production run. They can be produced ahead of time, but they would be very expensive. Cost: $50 to $500 per press sheet.

c. *The proofreading process*

When proofing traditionally typeset material, photocopy the paste-up artboards, and make your proofreading suggestions on the photocopy. This will protect the camera-ready artwork. If you're proofing desktop published-artwork, indicate your suggestions right on the laser proofs.

It is best to work on a flat surface or drafting table with good lighting. Use a colored pencil, pen, or marker. Use the straight edge of a ruler or card to guide your eye along. You should keep several reference books nearby, including a good dictionary, a secretary's manual, and a thesaurus. Proofreaders use symbols as shown in Sample #32 to indicate errors or omissions. Sample #33 shows how a proofreader would indicate errors on typeset copy. After the type is perfect, it is forwarded to the next step in the production cycle.

With a pencil or marker in hand, scan the material quickly for obvious errors such as a wrong heading or address, wrong type style, and printing irregularities. Then, read carefully, letter by letter, for meaning, spelling, grammar, correct usage, and accuracy of information. Sometimes, the only error is a misplaced word or an omitted word, but the meaning can be changed quite drastically. Include punctuation marks in your checking. Mark errors with the correct proofreader's marks.

Don't rely on a computer software package to do your proofreading. Read the lines carefully; avoid confusion, ambiguity, racism, sexism, and stupidity. Also, watch for line breaks. Here are examples of poor line breaks:

GBC is an excellent cam-
pus.

Any good, qualified stud-
ent can attend college.

Too many hyphens in a row are almost as bad as poor hyphenation. Sometimes you can't avoid hyphenating, but it's never necessary to

SAMPLE #32
PROOFREADER'S MARKS

Description	Mark	Example
Take out letter, letters or words indicated	ℓ	He opened the window.
Insert space	#	He opened thewindow.
Turn inverted line	⊙	He opened the window.
Insert letter	e	He opned the window.
Set in lowercase	l.c.	He Opened the window.
Wrong font	wf	He opened the window.
Broken letter. Must replace	X	He opened the windo .
Reset in italic	ital.	He opened the window.
Reset in roman	roman	He opened the window.
Reset in bold face	bold	He opened the window.
Insert period	⊙	He opened the window
Transpose letters or words as indicated	tr.	He the opened window.
Let it stand as is. Disregard all marks	stet	He opened the window.
Insert hyphen	=/	He windowshopped.
Equalize spacing.	eq.#	He opened the window.
Move over to point indicated.	[	He opened the window.
[if to the left; if to the right]		
Lower to point indicated	⊔	He opened the window.
Raise to point indicated	⊓	He opened the window.
Insert comma	∧	Yes he opened the window.
Insert apostrophe	∨	He opened Janes window.
Enclose in quotation marks	⟨⟨ ⟩⟩	He opened the window.
Enclose in parenthesis	( )	He opened the window.
Enclose in brackets	[ ]	He opened the window.
Replace with capital letter	cap.	he opened the window.
Use small capitals instead of type now used	sc	He opened the window.
Draw the word together	⌒	He opened the window.
Insert inferior figure (subscript)	⋀	He got H2O.
Insert superior figure (superscript)	⋁	Macintosh® computers.
Used when words left out are to be set from copy	see copy	He the window.
The diphthong is to be used	ǣ	Caesar opened the window.
The ligature of these two letters is to be used	fl	He fled from the scene.
Spell out words marked with circle	spellout	He fled on the 2nd.
Start a new paragraph	⊄	to. He opened the window.
Should not be a paragraph. Run in	no ⊄	to. He opened the window.
Out of alignment. Straighten	=	He opened the window.
1-em dash	|⅟|	He opened the window
En dash	|⅟|	He opened the window
Indent 1 em	□	He opened the window.
Indent 2 ems	□□	He opened the window.
Query to author. A query is encircled.	opens?	He opened the window.
Flush left, ragged right	[	[He opened the window.
Centered	⊐[	] He opened the window.[
Flush right, ragged left	⊐	]He opened the window.
Justified	[⊐	[He opened the window.]

After the copy has been typeset, a proofreader will check it for spelling, grammar, punctuation, and style. Changes are indicated in the margin. If the typesetting is perfect it will be forwarded to the next department. If there are errors in the typeset copy, it will be returned to the typesetter for corrections.

[margin: justify]

Good copy Preparation

[margin: 12 pts (delete 12 pts. of space)]

[margin: typesetter]

When preparing copy for a typeseter or printer, it is important to supply clean copy. Copy should be typed on standard 8.5" x 11" bond paper, and on one side of the sheet only. Use a 6" column so that you have a generous margin. The type should be double-spaced. every page should contain the same number of lines. Make sure all pages are numbered consecutively to avoid confusion if the sheets get separated. Also, make sure the job title appears at the top of every page to prevent the copy from being mixed up with another job. Write your typesetting instructions clearly in the left-hand margin, using the standard set of proofreaders' marks. Learn these proofreading marks: they are brief, clear, and they convey your instructions efficiently. Most typesetters will follow only the instructions you give them; you cannot expect them to make design decisions. The responsibility for these decisions, and for clearly directing the typesetter, is yours and yours alone.

[margin: (Delete Space)]

[margin: lm 24 Should be flush left on a measure of 24 picas]

hyphenate three times in a row, or six lines in a paragraph. To eliminate a hyphen, you could change the sentence slightly or substitute another word.

Often, too many hyphens are the result of using a justified alignment (text aligned on both sides of a column) in a line that is too short for the point size. Can you change the text to left alignment? Can you adjust the letter or wordspacing, kern, widen the margin, or add spaces before the offending word on a justified line to bump it down to the next line?

Never hyphenate a word in a headline. Any headline can be broken at a logical point. Insensitive line breaks can also make your text awkward or ambiguous. Group lines of a heading into correct grammatical sections. Which of the following is more appropriate?

Diana's Fruit
Stand

or

Diana's
Fruit Stand

Fair in Metro
Toronto a huge success

or

Fair in Metro Toronto
a huge success

Watch line breaks in body text also. If most of the text you create is flush left with a ragged right margin, try to keep the right margin as even as possible. This will create a visual effect as well as smoother reading. You may have to bump words or rewrite copy.

Also, subheadings should not fall within three lines of the bottom of a page or column. When possible, avoid having them appear at the top of a page or column. Widow and orphan problems are best resolved editorially. The worst graphic horror is the subhead that stands alone with its following paragraph on the next page. Reducing or adding text can eliminate short lines or paragraphs. See the tips at the end of this chapter for additional details to watch for.

d. Checking color proofs

You've prepared a perfect design, and you've marked it up for press. Now you need to correct the proofed result. Usually a color separation house or commercial printer will provide a Dylux, match print, or color key for process color projects or two-color jobs before the printing stage. A press proof is made on the printing press with the actual plates and ink to be used.

Here are some tips on what to look for when checking color proofs:

(a) Repetitive backgrounds — If a common color or tint background is required for several pages in a newsletter, it may be difficult to maintain consistency across pages. For example, if a buff color is used in the background, it may consist of a percentage tint of process yellow. If some pages require a heavy weight of yellow to be run for the photos, the tints on those pages will be heavier than on the other pages. A special fifth color (a Pantone color) for the backgrounds only should prevent this problem. Remember, it is more expensive to run five colors than four.

(b) Mechanical tints — When specifying tints, give percentages of the process colors, which can be obtained from a tint chart. For example, specify 100% magenta and 100% yellow to create red. Avoid specifying tints with a Pantone color swatch or reference number to match, as many special colors cannot be obtained from the four-color process. The tint on the proof can be checked against the tint chart. Look for mottled tints, which can be caused by the film or plate being exposed out of contact. Watch for moiré, an undesirable pattern created when reproductions are made from halftones.

(c) Color bar — The color bar on the side of a process color page compares the amount of color used in the film and how much is used in the printing process. For example, if the proofer has used too much yellow ink, so that the proof looks too yellow even though the film is correct, the color bar will show this.

(d) Register — Check registration marks to see if the job has been proofed in register. If it is correct, all you will see is black. If it is out of register, the colors will show next to the black.

(e) Trim and bleed — Check trim marks for position and that the bleed allowance is correct.

(f) Flopping — When a photograph or illustration appears reversed left to right in a color proof, it should be marked "flop." This correction requires more than just turning the film over, because the emulsion would be on the wrong side and therefore out of contact with the plate. A new contact film should be made with the emulsion on the correct side.

(g) Fit — If the register marks fit, but you can see colors sticking out from the edge of the picture, the job has been planned out-of-fit.

TIPS FOR PROOFREADERS

- Check over each page and reference number carefully
- Double-check all other numbers
- Mistakes tend to be clustered, so if you find one, look for others around it
- Make sure the information is in the right sequence
- Notice paragraph lengths; note when they're too long (shorter is better)
- Check to see if writers' page and section references are accurate
- Check spelling, grammar, and punctuation
- Be sure that brackets, quotes, and parentheses are used correctly
- Watch for repeated words, like "the the"
- Look for missing words (often small ones like "a" or "the" are left out)
- Check for proper hyphenation
- Is the editorial content consistent?
- Do photographs and artwork have a cutline explaining the details of the photo?
- Do headlines reflect the article, or can you suggest an alternative?
- Check for style consistency. Check that italic or bold type is used consistently, but not overused.
- Recheck arithmetic in charts
- Check telephone numbers
- Check unsual or technical words
- Check names of people in photographs
- Check for sense
- Check that the style sheet has been followed

It is very difficult to catch all your errors, so have someone else proofread what you write. Here are some things to watch for when you're proof-reading.

16
Printing

After you have produced camera-ready artwork, you will want to produce multiple copies for distribution to your readers. If you have a small quantity, a photocopying machine will be satisfactory. If you require more than 1,000 copies, consider offset-lithography. If you print less than 1,000 copies, you may opt for instant printing with paper plates or photocopying. If you require more than 10,000 copies, use a web press, which prints on roll- or web-fed paper.

Printing is a means of reproducing an image from one surface to another using ink. The transfer of an image can be accomplished by one of the four conventional printing processes: offset-lithography, letterpress, gravure, and screen printing.

a. Dealing with printers

As a customer, you have the right to expect a quality product at a fair price. You also have the right to expect the following:

- Good, quality printing void of hickeys, smudges, and poor registration
- Knowledgeable, helpful assistance from staff
- Delivery within a reasonable length of time
- Accurate registration of spot or process colors
- Paper quality that meets your specifications and budget
- A reasonable price based on materials, expertise, and labor involved
- Consistency of ink from page to page, top to bottom (Sometimes, the ink color is darker at the top of the paper and lighter at the bottom.)
- Good quality finishing such as folding, trimming, drilling, and binding
- Proper exposure for halftones, negative film, and making plates

In return, printers deserve a customer's respect. As a customer, be prepared to —

- pay promptly. If you cannot pay cash when you pick up the finished job, establish payment terms with the manager before the job is run.
- provide vital information to the printer so he or she doesn't have to phone with questions. When you take a job to a print shop, attach a note specifying quantity, ink color(s), paper stock, bindery instructions, trim size, and other pertinent information about the job.

note specifying quantity, ink color(s), paper stock, bindery instructions, trim size, and other pertinent information about the job.

- supply the best photographs and artwork available. Printers cannot improve a blurry photo.

b. Offset-lithography

Seventy percent of printing today is done with offset-lithography. In lithography, ink is transferred from a flat-surfaced lithographic plate mounted around a cylinder to an intermediate, rubber-covered blanket cylinder. This blanket cylinder transfers the ink to the paper. Both ink and water are applied to the lithographic plate. The image area of the plate holds ink and repels water; the non-image area holds water and repels ink.

The offset-lithography method of printing can be used for newsletters, brochures, business forms, stationery, posters, and charts. Offset lithography produces the cleanest type.

c. Letterpress printing

Relief or letterpress printing transfers ink from a raised surface. With a "backward reading" raised type, it produces sharp, clean type. The raised surface holds the ink; the lower (etched out) surface does not. There is no water involved in letterpress.

The biggest advantage of the letterpress is that corrections can be made easier and less expensively since individual letters, lines of type, or engravings can be removed and replaced. Proofs can be pulled directly from the plate. These plates are very expensive to make but they can withstand long runs.

d. Gravure printing

In gravure printing, ink is transferred to the paper from hollows etched below the plate surface. The plate surface is inked and then scraped with a precision doctor blade; the paper then pulls the ink out of the hollows (cells). Related terms are intaglio, rotogravure, and photogravure.

Rotogravure is the best method for reproduction of color photographs or monotone halftones when speed is required. Gravure printing is not really suited for type or other linework, but it is excellent for reproducing art and color photographs.

Because the plates are very expensive and corrections are almost impossible, this press is uneconomical and impractical for short runs. It is used best for magazines, newspaper supplements, catalogues, books, advertising literature, and fine art reproductions.

Type produced by gravure printing has slightly ragged, saw-toothed edges, even on absorbent paper. These edges are caused by the cell walls on the plate cylinder.

e. Screen printing

Screen printing is the best process for printing in small quantities and on almost any surface such as paper, metal or glass, flat or curvilinear. The biggest disadvantage is the inability to do long press runs. Screen printing is not very good for producing halftones and process color projects.

Type produced in screen printing will show a fabric pattern. Screen printing is achieved by the use of a stencil. Non-printing areas are blocked with a non-porous material. The screen stencil prints solids similar to the line plate. The screen is placed in contact with the paper (or other printing surface), and a rubber squeegee forces the ink through the mesh in the screen.

f. Paper selection

The right paper can make the difference between an attractive and a mediocre newsletter.

Selecting the right paper is a combination of personal preference, the printing process, the design, and economic restrictions. The choice of paper color will be influenced by readability, impact, and the psychology of color.

Choose a paper color that will look good and be readable. Studies show that cream- or buff-colored paper reduces fatigue on readers. Printing on off-white paper, such as natural, cream, buff, or ivory, adds to the informality of communications.

Consider the cost of the paper as well. Although light colored paper costs a little more than white, it is more opaque. Dark colored paper costs substantially more than white and reduces the legibility of type. White is the least expensive paper because it is the most popular and is readily available.

Uncoated stock comes in a variety of colors, but there are few colored, coated papers. Glossy or coated stocks may produce a glare or reflection that, after time, may induce eyestrain or fatigue.

Choose a paper that will stand out. By using a non-standard paper color, you may add impact to your newsletter because the majority of publishers use white. Creams and tans are a safe choice; bright colors should be used with discretion.

Remember that printing on a colored stock with two colored inks can create the effect of a three-colored job without the expense.

When planning your newsletter schedule, remember that your printer may not have some colored papers in stock. Custom orders may take a few days.

Your newsletter's content may dictate the choice of paper color. Environmental or agricultural newsletters will probably choose earth tones: tan, light gray, or soft green. If you produce a company publication, it may be a reflection of your company's corporate colors and identity.

If in doubt about the choice of paper, contact a printer or paper merchant. They can show you printed samples that will provide a good indication of what you can expect from any given paper.

1. Printability

Printability is determined by a paper's absorbency and smoothness of the surface. When printing halftones, the quality of the image will depend on how accurately each dot prints.

If you've ever tried a less expensive paper in your laser printer, you've probably noticed how the characters bleed or spread because of the surface or finish of the paper.

Often, the more expensive the paper is, the better your color control will be.

There are two kinds of paper: coated and uncoated. Usually coated (or glossy) stock is less absorbent and more expensive. Because it is less absorbent, a printer usually prints slightly slower, so the paper can absorb the ink. Being less absorbent, it can hold a smaller dot, which will not blend into other colors. Most magazines use a glossy stock and a finer halftone (more dots per inch in a photograph). White is the most popular color of coated stock, but other colors are available.

Uncoated stock with a dull finish comes in any color. Sometimes the color of the paper and the inks you use may offer undesirable results.

The surface or finish of the paper is important; a smooth paper will produce uniform, accurate images with good detail, contrast, and color. If the dots of a halftone or fine strokes of type will not print accurately, then the printed image will lack strength and detail.

2. Colored stock

Consider a colored stock for these reasons. If most printing is on white paper, messages on color stock get attention. Color stimulates positively and negatively. Stock can create atmosphere and build retention. Black and white lacks the psychological impact of printing color ink on color stock. Paper and ink manufacturers have developed compatible combinations of colored ink on paper.

If you've been using a second color ink to get a bit of color into your newsletter, try changing the color of the paper stock instead.

Some publications have a second ink color on the front page to differentiate between issues. Changing the paper stock does not increase costs, but a second spot color does because it requires an additional printing plate and more time for press clean-up and accurate registration.

g. Bindery

Binding and finishing operations shape the final printed piece including fastening the pages together to form a book or to protect them.

1. Cutting

Paper cutting, done before printing, cuts large sheets of paper to press size. This can be done by a hand-lever cutter (used in small commercial shops) or on a large, power-operated cutter found in large, commercial printing houses.

Most printing houses have machines that fold sheets many different ways. Sample #34 shows how an eight-page newsletter would be folded. If you have a large run, consider an automated folding-stuffing-sealing machine, such as the System One Folder Inserter distributed by Alcatel Friden. This machine can automatically fold 900 sheets, insert them into envelopes, and then moisten and seal the flaps in one hour. Smaller folding machines are also available.

2. Collating

Collating gathers parts of a job in a regular sequence such as the pages of a booklet. This is done before binding operations. Many larger binderies have automated equipment for collating. Small printing shops manually collate by walking around a table and inserting one folded page inside the next folded page.

The standard size newsletter has a finished size of 8½" x 11". It is usually produced from one 11" x 17" sheet to create a four-page newsletter. An eight-page newsletter is created from two 11" x 17" sheets, which are folded, and the inside sheet inserted or collated into the outside sheet.

3. Drilling and punching

Drilling and punching operations make holes in the paper for binding into a ring binder, metal, or plastic device.

Three holes are drilled into many newsletters so they can be stored in a three-ring binder. The three holes may encourage readers to save the document. If you can't afford the extra cost of having your newsletter drilled, you could print small circles on your newsletter and the readers can punch their own holes.

4. Stitching and stapling

Fastening the pages together is called binding, and often includes a cover. Most newsletters, booklets, small pamphlets, and magazines use wire staples. Most use saddle stitching, while others are side stitched. If your publication has more than eight pages and is folded and collated, you could have two staples saddle stitched into the middle fold to hold all the pages together.

If your publication is printed on lose sheets of standard paper, you will want to side stitch them by having a staple added on the left side. Side stitching can use one, two, three, or more staples down the side of your sheets.

h. Recycling

Many coated paper stocks are recyclable. In fact, coated paper is a desired component in making recycled newsprint, because it improves brightness, opacity, and strength. Some experts predict a severe shortage of old coated magazines and newsletters in the near future as waste paper recovery rates increase sharply.

If a publication is perfect-bound or has a UV-coated cover, it is not recyclable. There are some UV coatings and binder glues that claim to be

IMPOSITION OF A NEWSLETTER

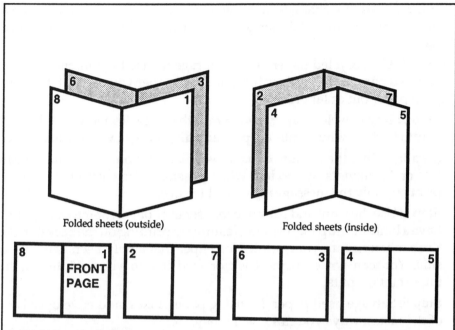

Folded sheets (outside)　　　　　　Folded sheets (inside)

Imposition for an eight-page newsletter.
Newsletters with multiples of four pages, such as four, eight, or twelve pages, may be printed on 11" x 17" paper, that are folded. Each sheet of 11" x 17" paper has two pages printed on each side of the sheet to create four pages per sheet. An eight-page newsletter would have two sheets of 11" x 17" paper—after folding, the inside pages would be inserted inside the outside pages.

For example, pages one and eight would be printed on one side of the sheet, and then pages two and seven would be printed on the back. Pages four and five are printed on one side of another sheet, and then pages three and six would be printed on the other side.

8 + 1	(9)
2 + 7	(9)
6 + 3	(9)
4 + 5	(9)

Notice how even-numbered pages are always on the left, and odd-numbered pages are always on the right. The page numbers of each page of a spread total one more than the number of pages in the publication.

This formula is true for any publication. If you had a 64-page book, all of the spreads would total 65 (one more than the number of pages in the book).

If you are printing more than 2,000 copies of your newsletter, the printer may choose to print "four-up" on larger sheets of paper, as demonstrated below. After printing, the newsletter would be folded twice and trimmed to create eight pages.

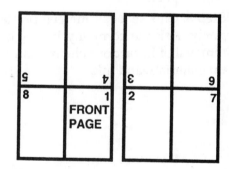

"environmentally friendly," but whether recycling plants can deal effectively with these items is another question.

Environmentally sound production and printing won't cost you much, and requires few changes in the way you work. Here are eight steps to initiating environmental changes in the simple actions you perform every day.

Step 1: Use recycled paper and encourage its use to your clients. Using recycled paper won't reduce the amount of paper you use, but it will help keep paper out of landfills.

Step 2: Buy recycled paper from a mill that recycles its waste. The only way to find out which mills are properly disposing of waste is to ask them.

Step 3: Reduce the amount of paper you use. Edit on screen and transmit text or documents by modem when possible. Use electronic mail, and print out only the messages you need to save.

Step 4: Use the front and back of every sheet of paper. Some laser printers have a built-in "duplex" printing feature for printing on the back of pages. Keep a box next to your printer for paper that's only been used on one side. You can write on the back or feed it into your printer for less important outputs.

Step 5: Salvage used paper. Re-using paper, faxes, and envelopes is one of the easiest ways you can save money.

Step 6: Recharge or recycle laser printer toner cartridges. By recharging a toner cartridge you pay between $40 and $60, while a new cartridge can cost twice as much. Some cartridge manufacturers strongly advise against used recharged cartridges because they won't provide "optimal performance."

Step 7: Purchase from mail-order companies that use recycled packing material. Before ordering a package by mail, ask if they have a recycling program or use recyclable packing material. One company I know packs with popcorn.

Step 8: Choose a commercial printer that handles hazardous chemicals safely. Ask the company if they comply with regulations for the safe removal of hazardous chemicals such as photographic chemicals, clean-up materials, and ink.

HOW TO CUT COSTS AT THE PRINTERS

- Buy paper in quantity.
- Use standard paper sizes, colors, and weights.
- Obtain estimates from several designers, typesetters, printers, and paper suppliers.
- If you have the same spot color for every issue, you can have it printed in advance and stored at the print shop. (For example, if you preprint a year's supply of your blue nameplate then you will just have to print the black ink for each issue.)
- Obtain a contract for services for long periods. A printer may give you a better rate if you commit yourself for a year.
- Since most standard newsletters are printed on 11" x 17" paper and folded to create four pages, always think in groups of four. If you have more than four pages, keep page counts in multiples of four.
- Use lighter-weight paper.
- Ask your printer if he or she has any paper in storage that can be used. You may get a good rate.
- Every change or correction after the printer has the artwork costs money, so proofread carefully before sending to the printers.
- If a supplier offers a discount for prompt payment, take advantage of it.
- Deliver work on time to avoid overtime charges. Enforce deadlines; delays cost money.
- Don't pay for any artwork or printing that is inferior. If it's not what you asked for, have it re-done.

17
Distribution

After your newsletter has been printed and finished, it must be distributed to your readers. Employee publications can establish their own methods of distribution to employees. Postal distribution is the most popular way of getting your newsletter into the hands of readers.

a. Stuffing and sealing envelopes

Since first class mail rates are higher for larger envelopes, it would be a good idea to use smaller No. 10 envelopes for mailing your newsletter. If you have a newsletter that is folded in half to a finished size of 8½" x 11", can your printer also fold the newsletter twice to fit into a business envelope? Many small commercial printers can only fold one way, and cannot fold the newsletter again.

If you have a small run, you and your volunteers can manually fold and stuff newsletters into envelopes. With the use of a bottle moistener or a roll-on moistener, you can also manually seal the envelopes.

If you have a large run, consider an automated folding-stuffing-sealing machine, such as the System One Folder Inserter distributed by Alcatel Friden mentioned in the previous chapter. This machine can fold 900 sheets, insert them into envelopes, and moisten and seal the flaps in one hour.

b. Addressing

If your publication qualifies for reduced bulk rates, you will have to type the address in all caps without punctuation:

ATTN: DR JOE SMITH
NAME OF DEPARTMENT
NAME OF COMPANY
123 ANY STREET
YOUR CITY
PROVINCE/STATE Z1P 0G0

Post offices can sort mail more efficiently when addresses can be read by optical character recognition (OCR). The last line of the address should be one inch from the bottom of the envelope or address panel. You need good contrast between ink and paper and the address should align with the edge of the envelope, and not be skewed. Optical character recognition requires a standard typeface and plenty of space between letters, words, and lines, but does not require punctuation. The city, province or state, and postal code should be on the last line. Use standard two-letter abbreviations for provinces and states. For subscription newsletters, you will want to add the expiration date so you and the reader know when the subscription expires.

Sometimes the most difficult task of publishing a newsletter is maintaining an accurate and up-to-date mailing list. If you mail your publication to hundreds of readers, you are probably maintaining a database or mailing list on your computer. With a database program, the addresses can be sorted alphabetically, by region, by expiry date, or by postal code. A database program should help you maintain and sort the mailing list.

The mailing list can be printed onto sheets of self-adhesive address labels that fit into your laser printer or dot matrix printer. You could also purchase an easy-to-operate label printer to connect to your computer to produce adhesive labels that can be peeled from the backing paper and placed on envelopes.

For larger distributions, consider an automated address printer that prints an address directly onto the envelope without the use of pressure sensitive labels. The Direct Impression Address Printer manufactured by Friden Neopost will print up to 3,000 pieces per hour.

If you have a huge mailing list, consider the services of a letter service or lettershop that specializes in addressing, lists, and distribution.

c. *Postage*

If your newsletter is mailed to readers, how do you apply the postage to the envelope? For small quantities, you could buy rolls of stamps, wipe the back across a wet sponge and stick each one onto the envelope.

Rather than sticking hundreds of postage stamps individually, consider a mailing machine. Some postage machines, such as the Friden Neopost 9000 Mailing Machine, will seal envelopes, stamp them, and stack the mail at a rate of 40 per minute.

As your circulation increases, you will want to take advantage of reduced bulk mail rates. To qualify for reduced rates, check with your postal services representative. As well, decide on whether you want first, second, or third class mail, bearing in mind that first class costs more and delivers faster than third class.

d. *Other methods of distribution*

If you prefer not to use a postal service, there are other ways to distribute your newsletter.

1. Handouts

Newsletters left in lunchrooms or on store counters do not enjoy a high readership since many are thrown out.

If you distribute your newsletters door to door, don't leave them in mailboxes, since you could be fined. It's not worth the hassle. You could pay for door-to-door delivery, but it can be uncertain or expensive.

2. Piggybacks

Your publication could be delivered in an envelope along with a paycheck or invoice. Be cautious about the increased weight and postage rates of the mailing piece.

3. Modem mix

If you have to have to ship 400 copies of your newsletter to another city, consider sending your newsletter by modem from your computer to a computer in that city. That city location could print the copies and distribute them for less than the cost of shipping.

If you distribute by modem, consider a format that allows local editors to add stories or graphics. Local news could use a one-page insert or fill space deliberately left blank.

e. *Circulation*

Depending upon your marketing objectives, you may wish to launch a new publication or increase the mailing list of your current newsletter. If your newsletter is distributed to potential clients, dealers, other businesses, or by subscription, your objective may be to increase the circulation, thereby increasing sales opportunities.

The Canadian Chapter of the Newsletter Publishers Association compiles an annual directory of the Canadian newsletter industry. A free listing is available to members and non-members. Mail information about your newsletter to:

Newsletter Publishing Association
c/o MPL Communications Inc.
133 Richmond Street West
Toronto, Ontario
M5H 3M8

Other newsletter directories:

Newsletters in Print
Gale Research Inc.
835 Penobscot Building
Detroit, MI 48226-4094

Oxbridge Directory of Newsletters
Oxbridge Communications, Inc.
150 Fifth Avenue, Suite 636
New York, NY 10011

You can increase your newsletter circulation with direct mail. The average person receives about 300 direct mail packages in the mail every year. Your package must compete for attention.

Since your package must compete with hundreds of others, you need teaser copy and graphics on the envelope to entice the reader to open it. Window envelopes are effective attention-getters, as is large, shouting type. Tearaways and polybags encourage readers to get involved. The accompanying letter should be two to four pages in length. Use a headline and subheads to draw attention to important parts of the letter. Italic or bold type and underlining can add emphasis.

The business reply card or envelope closes the sale and gets the reader to take action. The selling copy must be persuasive. A reply card or envelope definitely increases the number of responses.

The reply card could be a perforated part of the letter, brochure, or stand alone. Repeating a photo or color from the brochure or letter will help unite all of the items of your package.

Direct marketing studies have revealed that business reply envelopes do increase the number of responses received. Reply envelopes attract pranks, however, and this upsets a few small mailers.

Business Access is a free publication that contains articles on business, promotion, banking, retail, and some legal advice. To receive a free copy, write to:

Business Access
P.O. Box 4850, Station E
Ottawa, Ontario
K1S 9Z9

TIPS TO INCREASE YOUR READERSHIP

- Send a press release to the media.
- Write articles in related magazines.
- Send copies by direct mail to the target audience.
- Insert reply card or subscription form in newsletter.
- Distribute copies at related association meetings.
- Bulk mailing to local businesses.
- Distribute copies at related trade shows or events.
- Be a guest speaker at related meetings or events.
- Insert your newsletter into related publication.
- Mail out postage-paid business reply cards inviting recipients to send for complimentary issue.
- Hang flyers in strategic locations.
- Promote a seminar or open house.

Here are a few methods of increasing the potential readership of your newsletter.

OTHER TITLES BY
SELF-COUNSEL PRESS

HOW TO INTERVIEW
The art of the media interview
by Paul McLaughlin

Professional interviewers — on radio, TV, and in print — make interviewing look so easy. How do they do it? Does being a good interviewer depend on having the "right" personality? Or is it simply a matter of learning a set of techniques that guarantee success every time?

Author Paul McLaughlin draws on the experience of the professionals to examine the art of effective listening, the importance of reseach, pointers on obtaining interviews, how to prepare questions, and the specialized requirements of print and broadcast interviews. A highlight of each chapter is the feature interview with well-known interviewers such as Patrick Watson, George Plimpton, and Barbara Frum. $9.95

Some of the topics explored in this book are:

- where to track down research material
- how to line up interviews
- how to use other sources to develop a profile of the interviewee
- why you shouldn't be afraid of silence
- how tone of voice can affect your interview
- the best locations to choose for your interview

PRACTICAL TIME MANAGEMENT
How to get more things done in less time
by Bradley C. McRae

Here is sound advice for anyone who needs to develop practical time management skills. It is designed to help any busy person, from any walk of life, use his or her time more effectively. Not only does it explain how to easily get more things done, it shows you how your self-esteem will improve in doing so. More important, emphasis is placed on maintenance so that you remain in control. Whether you want to find extra time to spend with your family or read the latest bestseller, this book will give you the guidance you need — without taking up a lot of your time! $7.95

Some of the skills you will learn are:

- Learning to monitor where your time goes
- Setting realistic and attainable goals
- Overcoming inertia
- Rewarding yourself
- Planning time with others
- Managing leisure time
- Finding time for physical fitness
- Planning time for hobbies and vacations
- Maintaining the new you

MOTIVATING AND MANAGING TODAY'S VOLUNTEERS
How to build and lead a terrific team
by Flora MacLeod

People volunteer to contribute in a meaningful way to the community. Yet many new and long-time volunteers end up quitting; they feel their ideas and expertise are neither considered nor valued. Managing volunteers and making sure they feel they are full-fledged contributors to the organization is a full-time job. This book will help you hire a volunteer program manager and set up a program that organizes, evaluates, and recognizes your volunteers. $11.95

- Learn why organizations that haven't used volunteers before are now seeking them out

- Discover how a program manager can help keep volunteers organized and productive

- Take the steps to finding and hiring the ideal manager for your group's volunteer program

- Learn how to keep track of your current volunteers

- Attract the right volunteers to your organization

COMMENTS

Any comments you have on this or any other Self-Counsel publication are welcome. Please use space below.

_____

_____

_____

_____

_____

_____

_____

_____

ORDER FORM

All prices are subject to change without notice. Books are available in book, department, and stationery stores. If you cannot buy the book through a store, please use this order form. (Please print)

Name _____

Address _____

_____

Charge to: ❏ Visa   ❏ MasterCard

Account Number _____

Validation Date _____

Expiry Date_____

Signature_____

❏ **Check here for a free catalogue.**

IN CANADA

Please send your order to the nearest location:
Self-Counsel Press
1481 Charlotte Road
North Vancouver, B. C.
V7J 1H1

Self-Counsel Press
4 Bram Court
Brampton, Ontario
L6W 3R6

IN THE U.S.A.

Please send your order to:
Self-Counsel Press Inc.
1704 N. State Street
Bellingham, WA 98225

ON THE INTERNET
http://www.swifty.com/scp/

YES, please send me:

_____copies of **How to Interview**, $9.95

_____copies of Practical Time Management, $7.95

_____copies of Motivating and Managing **Today's Volunteers**, $11.95

Please add $3.00 for postage & handling. Canadian residents, please add 7% GST to your order.
WA residents, please add 7.8% sales tax.